PROGRAMMING IN FORTRAN

PROGRAMMING

STRUCTURED PROGRAMMING WITH

Vladimir Zwass

in FORTRAN

FORTRAN IV AND FORTRAN 77

BARNES & NOBLE BOOKS
A DIVISION OF HARPER & ROW, PUBLISHERS
New York, Cambridge, Hagerstown,
Philadelphia, San Francisco, London,
Mexico City, São Paulo, Sydney

ABOUT THE AUTHOR

Vladimir Zwass received his Ph.D. in computer science from Columbia University in 1975. He is currently an associate professor and chairman of the Computer Science Committee at Fairleigh Dickinson University. He was previously a member of the professional staff of the International Atomic Energy Agency in Vienna, Austria. As a consultant, he has advised, among other companies, Citibank and the Metropolitan Life Insurance Company.

Professor Zwass is the author of *Introduction to Computer Science,* a companion volume in the Barnes & Noble Outline Series and has contributed to professional journals. He is a member of the Association for Computing Machinery, IEEE, Sigma Xi and Eta Kappa Nu.

PROGRAMMING IN FORTRAN. Copyright © 1981 by Vladimir Zwass.

All rights reserved. Printed in the United States of America. No part of this book may be used or reproduced in any manner whatsoever without written permission except in the case of brief quotations embodied in critical articles and reviews. For information address Harper & Row, Publishers, Inc., 10 East 53rd Street, New York, N.Y. 10022. Published simultaneously in Canada by Fitzhenry & Whiteside Limited, Toronto.

FIRST EDITION

Designed by Charlotte Staub

Library of Congress Cataloging in Publication Data

Zwass, Vladimir.
   Programming in FORTRAN.
   (College outline series; CO/194)
   Bibliography: p.
   Includes index.
   1. FORTRAN (Computer program language)
2. Electronic digital computers—Programming. I. Title.
QA76.73.F25Z86   001.64′24   80–7763
ISBN 0–06–460194–3 (pbk.)

---

89 90   10 9 8

CONTENTS

PREFACE

This is an introductory textbook on computer programming with the use of FORTRAN. It is designed for direct classroom use, for individual study, or as an aid to understanding concepts presented in the classroom. It is also meant to serve as a review book and as a reference manual. With one significant exception (that of tape and disk file processing, of interest to advanced programmers only), the full language is discussed.

As much as some textbooks would lead the student to believe it, one does not become a programmer by learning a programming language statement by statement. One must learn to design the algorithm on which the program is to be based, to use the programming language in a methodical fashion to express thoughts rather than code in a helter-skelter manner, and to furnish a fully documented program. The best time to learn good programming habits is when one begins to program.

Thus, the emphasis here is on (1) methodical, structured design and the implementation of programs, and (2) the use of standard FORTRAN, which provides students with a transferable skill and allows them to create programs that are portable from one computer to another.

Students will learn how to design an algorithm via stepwise refinement of their initial idea of the problem solution. Both pseudocode and flowcharts are discussed as tools for algorithm design. (To the student who uses this text for self-instruction, I might say that I find pseudocode simpler and more pleasing to use.) The skill of algorithm design, once acquired, is applicable to programming in any language.

Since its initial development in the years 1954–57, FORTRAN (an acronym for "formula translation") has been greatly expanded and has become a widely used general-purpose language. The many software translators written for it have provided ever new and modified features that have eventually made it difficult to transfer a program from one computer installation to another. To facilitate program portability, the first voluntary FORTRAN standard was introduced in 1966. This standard corresponds to the FORTRAN IV version of the language.

The needs of non-numeric areas of application and the growing sophistication of programming practices led to the adoption in April 1978 of a new FORTRAN standard. This new standard, called FORTRAN 77, is based to a large degree on the WATFOR and WATFIV compilers for the language. Like the previous standard, FORTRAN 77 defines the full language and the subset language. The latter is rather close to the full language of the old standard. This book is based on the full FORTRAN 77 language.

FORTRAN 77 essentially incorporates FORTRAN IV, while it extends it in certain areas and clarifies certain ambiguities. Thus, almost any FORTRAN IV program will run correctly under a FORTRAN 77 system (but not vice-versa, of course).

The main innovations of FORTRAN 77 are list-directed input/output, block IF constructs, string processing with CHARACTER data, more general definitions of arrays and DO loops, and an extension of the capabilities for external file processing.

For a certain time, FORTRAN IV and FORTRAN 77 will coexist. The presentation offered in this book permits the programmer to use the systems based on FORTRAN IV and to take advantage of FORTRAN 77 facilities as well. The programming examples are presented with this point in mind. Certain instructions are also given for the use of WATFOR and WATFIV compilers.

▷ When the feature being described distinguishes FORTRAN 77 from FORTRAN IV or is available only in FORTRAN 77, the description is set off with triangular markers as illustrated here, unless the section heading makes this distinction clear. ◁

In general, the programmer should strive to conform to the standard to make the program more readable and to ensure its portability. Therefore, the presentation in this book is based directly on American National Standard FORTRAN (X3.9-1978).

The programmer should design programs of clear structure, with clear and concise documentation through use of pseudocode or flowcharts, and through uniform commenting. Several complete programs are offered as examples.

Good programming practices are pointed out throughout the text; they appear inside boxes, as shown here.

This volume may be used as a textbook in a one-semester programming course. It applies to the CS1 and CS2 courses of the Association for Computing Machinery Curriculum '78. A companion book in such courses, also in the Barnes & Noble Outline Series, is the author's *Introduction to Computer Science*. Two sources of problems with extensive commentaries are recommended in the bibliography at the end of the book.

I wish to thank my colleagues and students for creating the environment needed for the preparation of this work; I am particularly grateful to Professor Abe Lockman of Rutgers University for his kind cooperation. My thanks also go to Jeanne Flagg of Barnes & Noble for her expert editorial assistance and to Janet Goldstein of Harper & Row for her superb efforts in seeing the book through production.

Vladimir Zwass

INTRODUCTION
TO THE COMPUTER

Computers as we know them today emerged in the 1940s. Since then they have entered most fields of human activity as tools for the processing and storage of information.

A computer is not an independent problem solver. Its operation is directed by a program constituted of a sequence of instructions. If we change the program, the function of the computer also changes. Thus, computers are general-purpose information processors.

Basic components of a computer system are the central processing unit (CPU), main and secondary memories, and input/output devices. In addition to this hardware, systems software is provided; that is a set of service programs that make it easier for users to run their programs.

The central processor of a computer is only able to execute instructions expressed in a binary code called the machine language of the computer. Programs are almost never written in this code: the tedium would be unbearable. It is much easier to program in the assembly language of the given computer; again, a considerable effort is required of the programmer, however, toward the management of the machine resources.

Higher level languages, such as FORTRAN, on the other hand, permit the programmer to concentrate on the problem itself and to express the solution in a readable fashion. Before a program written in such a language may be executed, translation into the machine language is needed. This is performed by the computer itself under the control of a systems program, a translator. In the case of FORTRAN, the program is usually translated fully before execution is begun. The translator that performs this task is called a compiler.

A. WHAT A COMPUTER IS

A *computer* is a data-processing machine or, more generally, a machine for the manipulation of symbols. These symbols represent information of various kinds, for example, a number or a name.

In its operation, the computer is directed by a *program,* that is, a sequence of *instructions* that determine the operations to be carried out by the machine. The program is the procedure for obtaining the desired results. To obtain the results, most programs require *data.*

EXAMPLE 1–1

(a) A program may be written to compute the square root of a non-negative number.

The data item needed in this case is the number whose root is to be calculated. Thus, the program is general enough to compute the root of *any* number greater than or equal to 0; the data make the program specific to the task at hand.

(b) A program may be written to write mail solicitation letters in which the name and address of the prospect are inserted onto a preprinted form.

The file of names and addresses comprise the data for this program. These data are non-numeric; they are text (character) data.

Computers are universal: change the program, and instead of computing the square root of a number, the computer will produce the solicitation letters. Thus, the function of the computer at any moment is determined by the program it is executing.

The data make the program specific. Therefore, a program applies to a class of problems: it may be computing the square root of 15 or of 155.

B. ORGANIZATION OF A COMPUTER

1. FLOW OF INFORMATION IN A COMPUTER

The capabilities (and cost) of computer systems vary widely. Their basic organization is, however, the same. Thus, a computer system includes a number of functionally separate devices that constitute its *hardware.* These comprise the *central processing unit (CPU),* at which the program instructions are directed, the memory subsystem, where the instructions and data are stored, and *input* and *output devices* for communication with the environment of the system.

The flow of information in a computer system is shown in Fig. 1–1.

An input device receives the information and places it in the *main memory* (memory is often called *storage*). The CPU of the computer actually executes the instructions by applying them to data (with the use of its arithmetic-logic unit) and by directing the operation of other system units.

The intermediate and final results are stored in the main memory. As the execution of the program is progressing, the results may be communicated

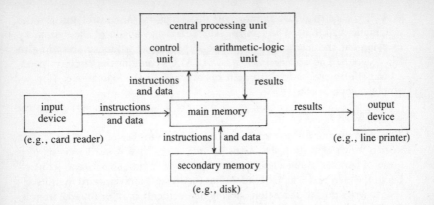

FIGURE 1-1. Flow of information in computer systems

to the outside world via an output device. They may also be stored in memory, until the program has been fully executed, to be presented all at once.

Programs and/or data may be stored in memory for extensive periods of time in order to avoid introducing them repeatedly from an input device. To provide a large memory capacity at a reasonable cost, cheaper and slower *secondary memory* devices are used. Before the information stored there is brought to the attention of the CPU, it has to be transferred to the main memory.

For technological reasons, all the information handled by a computer system is encoded internally as a string of 0's and 1's, i.e., in binary representation.

All the system components are electronic, with the exception of input/output and most of the secondary memory devices. (These devices have mechanical elements.)

The following sections describe the components of a computer system in detail sufficient for programming in a higher level language such as FORTRAN.

2. CENTRAL PROCESSING UNIT

The central processing unit (CPU) of the computer is designed to "comprehend" elementary instructions expressed in binary code. Three examples of such instructions are: add two numbers; compare two numbers and indicate the larger one; carry out the next instruction from a given memory location. This instruction code constitutes the *machine language* of the given computer.

A CPU consists of two functionally distinct parts: the control unit and the arithmetic-logic unit. The *control unit* directs the action of the system by carrying out the instructions and establishing their sequence according to the program. The *arithmetic-logic unit* (ALU) contains the circuitry needed to perform the basic arithmetic operations and the logical ones (for example, a comparison).

3. MEMORY

The main memory of a computer consists of a number of *locations,* called *words,* which contain instructions or data items. Every word consists of a uniform number of bits (holding 0 or 1) and has a unique *address,* its number in the memory. The CPU identifies (addresses) a given word in order either to *write* into this location, storing new contents in it, or to *read* from it, fetching the contents of the word without erasing them. In this manner, the CPU can obtain the instructions and data for the program and subsequently store the results in memory.

From the programmer's viewpoint, the main memory has the structure shown in Fig. 1–2.

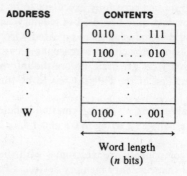

FIGURE 1–2. Programmer's view of the main memory

In order to extend the capacity of the main memory at a reasonable cost, computer systems usually have secondary (auxiliary) memories, selected from cheaper and slower types of storage than the main ones. Programs and data that are not expected to be needed soon by the CPU are stored there. The items contained in the secondary storage are usually accessible to the CPU only following their transfer to the main memory.

A typical secondary memory device is a magnetic disk. Much slower is a magnetic tape drive, also used.

4. INPUT/OUTPUT DEVICES

A number of various input/output (I/O) devices serve the need of the computer system for communication with the environment.

The most widely used input devices include card readers and the keyboards attached to display or printing terminals. Output is most often displayed on a cathode ray tube (CRT) screen, similar to a television tube, or on a line printer, which prints one line (rather than a single character) at a time.

5. SYSTEMS SOFTWARE

The intermediary between computer users and hardware is *systems software,* a set of programs that belongs to the configuration of a given computer system and facilitates its use. The programs written by the computer users are called *application software.*

A user of the computer, during the process of program design and implementation, called *programming,* must specify the operations to be performed by the computer. Natural languages, like English, used for human communication, are not fit for programming because of their ambiguity and lack of precision. On the other hand, programming in a machine language would be exceedingly tedious and would limit the applicability of programs, since they are not easily transferable to a different computer in this form (see Section C).

Users, therefore, program in *programming languages,* which must be translated into machine language. The computer itself performs this translation under the control of a systems program, a *translator.*

A program submitted to a computer system constitutes a *job* to be performed and requires the use of system resources, both hardware and software. The latter include the translators as well as *utility programs* (for example, sorting routines) that have been written by systems programmers rather than by the users. In order to assign the needed resources to a program and to mediate between the demands made by various users, a special systems program is required. This program, which manages all of the system resources, including the users' programs, is called a *supervisor, executive,* or *operating system.*

Extensive programs are required to manage data stored in some computer systems and to facilitate remote communication between a user and the system or, frequently, between distantly located computers.

The operating system, along with language translators, programs for data management and telecommunication, and utility programs, constitute the essential systems software. User programs may be simpler due to the presence of this software.

C. HIGHER LEVEL LANGUAGES

As already explained, in order to perform a task, the computer follows a sequence of orders. These orders are presented in the form of program instructions.

It was also explained that the hardware of the computer or, more precisely, its central processor, "understands" only the instructions expressed in the machine language of the given computer model. A machine language instruction looks like this:

1000110010101110
(a 16-bit word is assumed)

A part of the instruction specifies the operation to be performed (e.g., add, compare), and another part gives the addresses of the memory locations that hold the operands involved.

Programming in such binary code is extremely cumbersome: the programmer has to remember all the addresses of data and the binary codes of all of the operations. To modify such a program is an arduous chore.

To simplify the programmer's work, every computer model (or series) has its own *assembly language,* a low level programming language that permits the programmer to refer to a data item with the use of a symbolic name (instead of a binary address) and to use mnemonic, easy to remember, operation codes.

For example, the instruction shown above may look, in the assembly language of this hypothetical machine, as follows:

ADD GROSS, SALES

An assembly language program is translated into machine language by a rather simple translator, called an assembler.

Low level programming languages have the advantage of efficient use of computer resources. They have, however, two essential disadvantages that significantly limit their use.

As a simple encoding of a machine language, assembly language is very remote from natural language and thus difficult to use. Since every instruction specifies an elementary operation, long and hard-to-read programs result. Thus, assembly languages are rather demanding of the programmer's time.

Moreover, an assembly language is specific to a computer model. Therefore, the programs written in an assembly language are not *portable* from one computer model (or series) to another.

For these reasons, programming is predominantly performed in *higher level languages*. These allow the programmer to present the program in a terse and machine-independent fashion. The languages are problem-oriented rather than machine-oriented: very little knowledge of the machine organization is required. Moreover, programs written in a higher level language are portable, although minor modifications may be required (see Section D).

The most commonly used general-purpose higher level languages, along with FORTRAN, are BASIC, COBOL, Pascal, and PL/I. The general facilities of these languages are to a significant degree similar; thus a solid knowledge of FORTRAN programming will make it rather simple to learn other languages.

D. HOW A PROGRAM IS PROCESSED

Since computers cannot directly execute the instructions of a higher level language program, it has to be translated before execution. A FORTRAN program is usually translated fully before its execution begins; such translation is called compilation. A *compiler* is said to translate the *source program* (in a higher level language) into an *object program* (in machine language); see Fig. 1–3.

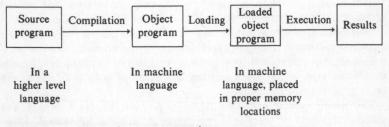

FIGURE 1–3. Stages of program processing

Another systems program, called a *loader*, then places the object program into the main memory locations assigned to it. The loaded object program is then executed.

As can be seen from the above discussion, what the computer does in response to a program written in a higher level language depends to a degree on the compiler for this language used to translate the program. The compiler together with the hardware of the computer constitute the *implementation* of the language. It is desirable to limit the differences between implementations: ideally, a FORTRAN program should be executed identically in any implementation and thus be fully portable. In practice, even though FORTRAN has been standardized, minor differences exist.

As an alternative to compilation, a higher level language program may be interpreted: translated and executed statement by statement. This is done rather infrequently in the case of FORTRAN (see Chapter 3–A).

2
ALGORITHMS AND THEIR PRESENTATION

Before writing a program in FORTRAN or any other programming language, the programmer should design the algorithm on which the program will be based.

An algorithm is a procedure for arriving at the required results with the use of the available data. An algorithm is more succinct than a program; thus it is easier to design the algorithm of a problem solution first, instead of taking an immediate plunge into the details of FORTRAN coding.

Moreover, algorithms may be designed in a top-down fashion via their stepwise refinement. First, a general outline of the problem solution is established; then it is refined (possibly in several stages) until the final form is obtained. Subsequently, the algorithm may be coded in FORTRAN or any other programming language.

Two widely used notations for algorithm presentation are flowcharts and pseudocode. Both of them lend themselves to stepwise refinement. Flowcharts are a graphical tool. Pseudocode is a textual description of the algorithm. It uses the same control structures that are employed in many higher level languages.

A deeper understanding of some of the structures presented in this chapter will be acquired during the study of Chapters 4 and 7. Modular design of algorithms is subsequently discussed in Chapter 8.

A. ALGORITHMS AND THEIR STEPWISE REFINEMENT

The first step to take in solving a problem with the use of a computer is to establish the procedure for arriving at the needed results using the available data. Such a procedure, if it can be carried out by a computer, is called an algorithm.

Thus, an *algorithm* is a sequence of instructions that, when carried out, will result in the solution of the problem (or the class of problems).

Since algorithms operate on data, both those initially given and those obtained during computation, the make-up of these data has to be established simultaneously with the design of the algorithm.

How do we specify an algorithm? To be presented to a computer, an algorithm has to be specified as a program. For all but the most trivial problems we do not, however, begin by specifying the algorithm in a programming language.

Programming languages, even the higher level ones (like FORTRAN) require minute attention to detail both in specifying the actual operations to be carried out and in observing the conventions of the language (a comma here, a parenthesis there). Programs with thousands of instructions are quite common. It is impossible to write such a program without first designing an accurate but more concise description of its operation. This description of the algorithm may then be refined, possibly in several stages until it may be converted into a program.

Algorithms are much easier to read than programs; they serve to communicate with people. Programs serve to give orders to computers.

The examples below show how very simple algorithms may be specified in English.

EXAMPLE 2-1

Problem

Determine the largest of three integers.

Algorithm: Initial Description

1. Compare the first and second integers and establish which is the larger one.
2. Compare the latter with the third integer; the larger is the result.

Thinking over this algorithm in more detail, we may refine this description as follows.

Algorithm: Refinement

1. Obtain (input) the first number; call it NUM1.
2. Obtain (input) the second number; call it NUM2.
3. Compare NUM1 with NUM2 and select the larger; if the numbers are equal, select NUM1. Call this number LARGE.
4. Obtain (input) the third number, call it NUM3,
5. Compare LARGE with NUM3 and select the larger; if the numbers are equal, select LARGE. Call this number LARGE.
6. Present (output) LARGE.
7. Stop.

Notes

Note that certain decisions in the design of an algorithm are made at the discretion of the designer (for example, step 4 may precede step 3; if two integers are equal in step 3, either may be selected). Other steps, however, cannot be changed without impairing the integrity of the algorithm (for example, step 4 must precede step 5).

EXAMPLE 2-2

A somewhat more complex problem is presented than that of the preceding example.

Problem

Determine the largest of N integers, where $N > 2$.

Analysis

Since the algorithm has to apply to any N greater than 2, N should be a parameter. Therefore, it will be one of the inputs to the program, along with the integers themselves.

Algorithm: Initial Description

1. Input N.
2. Input one by one N integers and keep the largest so far.
3. Output the kept integer.

Algorithm: Refinement

1. Input N.
2. Input first integer; call it NUM1.
3. Input second integer; call it LARGE.
4. Set up a counter of integers that have been read in; call it COUNT. Set COUNT equal to 2.
5. Compare NUM1 with LARGE; if NUM1 is greater than LARGE, set LARGE to equal NUM1. If COUNT equals N, output LARGE and stop; else increment COUNT by 1, input next integer, and call it NUM1; perform this step (step 5) again.

Notes

Note that this is not the intention of this problem to save the numbers in memory. Think about the way the numbers are called and the reason for this.

Follow through the algorithm with a few integers of your choice and convince yourself of its correctness.

The specification of algorithms in a natural language, like English, is increasingly ambiguous and inconvenient as the problems become more complex. Special algorithmic notations exist for the purpose. Two such notations, widely used, are flowcharts, a graphical method of algorithm specification, and pseudocode, somewhat easier to use and read. Both these notations are presented in the subsequent sections of this chapter. Before coding the program in a selected programming language, the programmer should design its algorithm in such a notation. Such an approach simplifies the design of programs. An algorithm presented in such a notation is also more readable than the program itself; it may serve to communicate with others or to you at a later time. Thus, such a description is a part of the *program documentation:* a set of written material that explains the program and makes it a finished product.

As noted above and as may be observed in the examples, the design of an algorithm progresses from a more general to a more detailed description.

This process of obtaining a detailed algorithm description from its initial general form is called *stepwise refinement*. Several stages of refinement may be needed; an algorithm is thus designed in a top-down fashion. The process stops when we are able to code directly from the algorithm.

Several examples of this process will be seen in this book.

B. FLOWCHARTS

A *flowchart* is a two-dimensional representation of an algorithm; the predefined graphic symbols of a flowchart are used to indicate the various operations and the flow of control.

The most significant feature of flowcharts is a clear presentation of the *flow of control* in the algorithm, i.e., the sequence in which the algorithm operations are performed.

A basic set of established flowchart symbols is presented in Fig. 2–1. Six of these symbols are *outlines* (also called boxes) of various shapes. When used in a flowchart, they contain appropriate wording. The wording is made more precise as the flowchart for a given problem solution is developed. The remaining symbol, the *flowline*, determines the sequencing among the tasks represented by the outlines.

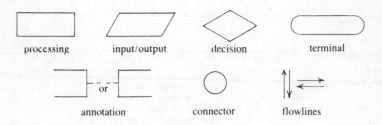

FIGURE 2–I. Flowchart outlines

The symbols have the following meaning:

processing: one or more computational tasks are to be performed sequentially;

input/output: data are to be read into the computer memory from an input device or data are to be passed from the memory to an output device;

decision: two alternative execution paths are possible; the path to be followed is selected during the execution by testing whether or not the condition specified within the outline is fulfilled;

terminal: appears either at the beginning of a flowchart (and contains the word "Start"), or at its conclusion (and contains "Stop");

annotation: contains comments that promote the understanding of the algorithm, or the description of data;

connector: makes it possible to separate a flowchart into parts; identical cross-reference symbols are placed in this outline where the flowline is interrupted and where it resumes;

flowlines: indicate the outline that is to be entered next.

A flowchart for the algorithm of Example 2–2 is presented in Fig. 2–2.

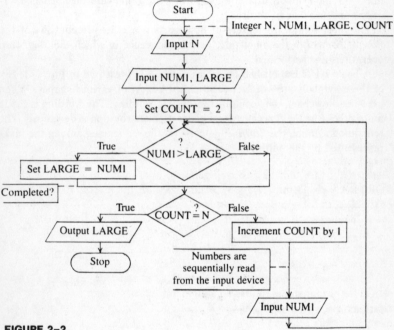

FIGURE 2–2.

If the flowchart were to be separated into two parts at the point marked X, the connectors would be used as shown in Fig. 2–3.

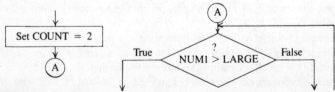

FIGURE 2–3.

Flowcharts allow the reader to follow the logic of the algorithm more easily than a linear description in English. The choice of the level of detail is at the discretion of the algorithm designer. During the refinement process more detail is gained.

An alternative to flowcharts, which does not require graphics, is discussed in the next section.

C. ESSENTIAL PROGRAMMING CONSTRUCTS AND PSEUDOCODE

1. PSEUDOCODE IN PROGRAMMING

An algorithmic notation that is preferred by many to flowcharts is pseudocode. *Pseudocode* is a notation in which the structures for the control of the execution flow are superimposed on the more or less formal descriptions of data manipulation. The main convenience of pseudocode is that it may be read as a text; no graphics are needed. At the same time, pseudocode clearly presents the flow of control in the algorithm.

The same basic control structures that are used in programming languages are also used in pseudocode. Thus, the essential structures are presented here; they will be better understood at a later time, when used in FORTRAN programming. Since pseudocode does not include formal specifications in the way programming does, various modifications of the forms shown here may be employed.

Both a pseudocoded algorithm and a program consist of a sequence of *statements:* orders for a computer action. A statement corresponds to a sentence in a text written in a natural language.

The task of every algorithm and program is to manipulate data. The means for data manipulation is an assignment statement: an order for a certain expression to be evaluated and the value obtained to be assigned to a named memory location.

To read data into the computer memory, input statements are needed. To write out the results, we require output statements.

In a pseudocode description of an algorithm, the assignments as well as the input and output statements (and, possibly, less formal orders) are expressed with the level of detail desired by the programmer. As the stepwise refinement process progresses, more precision is injected. To organize the computation in a logical order, control structures are used.

Three basic control structures are sequence (**begin-end**), decision (**if-then-else**), and loop (**while-do**).† These, sufficient to present any algorithm, constitute the fundamental means of a systematic programming process called

† In longhand, these keywords are usually underlined.

structured programming. Additional control structures may be used to simplify this process.

While these structures are not available directly in every higher level programming language (for example, in FORTRAN only some exist), it is possible to construct them using the statements of the given language. The programmer will find that thinking in terms of these structures will produce clearly organized programs that are easy to write, read, and modify.

Comments are needed in an algorithm and in a program to explain these to a reader.

As will be seen in Chapter 8, larger algorithms and programs may be organized into functionally separate modules. These modules are identified in the process of stepwise refinement and treated as separate algorithms. Modular programming significantly aids in design and comprehension of more complex programs.

2. DATA MANIPULATION

Computing consists of manipulating data. For example, an average of a set of integer numbers is obtained, or the names of employees are sorted in alphabetical order.

To manipulate a data item, we need to refer to it. It is most convenient to refer to a data item by a symbolic name. This name is associated by the software translator with the memory location where the value is stored. Such a named data item, whose value may vary during the program execution, is called a *variable.*

In Examples 2–1 and 2–2 we used several variable names. Note what an essential convenience this represents.

Aside from variables, fixed values, called *constants,* may be used in a program (or algorithm).

The kind of value that a variable may acquire depends on its *type.* Thus, we may have an integer or a character variable. The type of the variable determines also the operations that are applicable to it. (It does not make sense to add two names, does it?)

The types of the variables employed are specified by *type declarations* at the beginning of the program or algorithm.

To declare the type of two integer variables, for example, we will use a pseudocode statement (declaration):

Integer N, NUM

During the computation, a value may be given to a variable by an *assignment.* The general form of the assignment statement is

variable ← expression

where the arrow stands for "set to" or "assign." The expression is evaluated (the way expressions are evaluated in algebra), and the value is assigned to the variable.

EXAMPLE 2–3

(a) In the flowchart of Fig. 2–2, instead of saying

$$\text{Set COUNT} = 2$$

we could use the assignment

$$\text{COUNT} \leftarrow 2$$

(b) In the same flowchart, instead of saying

$$\text{Increment COUNT by 1}$$

we could use the assignment

$$\text{COUNT} \leftarrow \text{COUNT} + 1$$

As will be seen in Chapter 4, in FORTRAN the equal sign ($=$) is used to express assignment. The difference between the assignment and the algebraic equality should be, however, appreciated [look at the assignment in Example 2–3(b) above].

Note that if a variable name appears only in the expression on the right-hand side of the assignment statement, the value of the variable is not changed.

If the value of a variable is a part of the given data, it is read in from an input device, e.g.,

Input NUM1, LARGE

To present (e.g., print or display) the results, an output statement is necessary, e.g.,

Output LARGE

Comments, marked with initial asterisks, may be freely used to explain the algorithm. They do not influence the actions that will be carried out; they merely explain them. Comments are a necessary part of any algorithm or program.

EXAMPLE 2–4
The following is very simple.
  Problem
Add two integers and present their sum.

Algorithm

```
*SUM OF TWO INTEGERS IS OBTAINED
begin
  Input NUM1, NUM2;
  SUM ← NUM1 + NUM2;
  Output NUM1, NUM2, SUM *FOR ERROR CHECKING, ALL PRINTED*
end
```

The structuring of algorithms is discussed in the following subsection.

3. BASIC CONTROL STRUCTURES

There are three essential control structures in programming: sequence, decision, and loop. These suffice to express the logic of any algorithm. For ease of expression, additional control structures are also used.

A. SEQUENCE

If a number of statements is to be carried out in the order they are presented, this group of statements constitutes a *sequence*. To show this, the statements are enclosed between two delimiters, **begin** and **end**, as follows:

```
begin
  S₁;
  S₂;
  .
  .
  .
  Sₙ
end
```

The enclosed statements are indented for readability. Semicolons separate individual statements (the last one does not need a semicolon). Thus several statements may be placed on a single line.

The corresponding action may be expressed in the flowchart form as shown in Fig. 2–4.

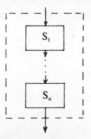

FIGURE 2–4. Sequence (**begin-end**) structure

Note that a complete algorithm constitutes a sequence of actions. It is therefore enclosed in **begin** and **end** delimiters.

Example 2–4 above illustrates the use of sequence.

B. DECISION

When the programmer needs to specify two alternative courses of action the decision construct is used. The choice of an alternative depends on the existence of a certain condition.

This construct expresses the following thought: "If a given condition exists, one action should be taken; otherwise the alternative action should be carried out."

This construct has the following form:

$$\textbf{if } C \textbf{ then}$$
$$S_1$$
$$\textbf{else}$$
$$S_2$$

where C is the condition (e.g., LARGE $>$ 5) and S_1 and S_2 are statements or groups of statements.

If the condition C is true, then statement (or group) S_1 is executed; otherwise, if C is false, S_2 is executed.

If S_1 and/or S_2 are groups of statements, they are enclosed in the **begin** and **end** delimiters.

The flowchart of the **if-then-else** construct is shown in Fig. 2–5.

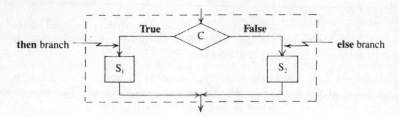

FIGURE 2–5. Decision (**if-then-else**) structure

EXAMPLE 2–5

The solution to the following problem will be developed throughout this section.

Problem

In a set of N integers, the positive numbers (including 0's) and the negative numbers are to be separately counted.

Use of Decision Construct

In order to process a given integer, the following statement will be incorporated in the algorithm:

if the integer is greater than or equal to 0 **then**
    increment the counter of positive integers by 1
else
    increment the counter of negative integers by 1

If the alternative to an action to be performed conditionally is no action, the **else** branch is empty (see this case in Example 2–7 below).

C. LOOP

The *loop* mechanism causes repeated execution of a sequence of statements while a certain condition is true. When the condition ceases to hold, control is passed to the statement following the last statement of the loop. Such repeated execution is called *iteration*.

If a loop is entered, the execution of the statements included in it should, after a finite time, cause the reversal of the condition that caused the entry. Otherwise an infinite loop would exist, representing a programming error. The program execution would have to be stopped by external means.

Several forms of this construct exist. The most useful is the **while-do** loop, whose general form is

while C **do**
S

where S is usually a group of statements delimited by **begin** and **end**.

The loop statement is executed as follows:

(1) Condition C is tested.
(2) If the condition exists, S is executed and control is returned to the **while** statement for the condition to be tested again; otherwise the statement following S is executed.

It follows from the above that the statements S should, after a certain number of iterations, reverse the condition C.

The flowchart of the **while-do** construct is shown in Fig. 2–6.

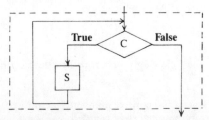

FIGURE 2–6.   Loop (**while-do**) structure

In Example 2–5 we need the following loop:

while fewer than N integers have been read in **do**
    begin
        read in the next integer;
        increment the appropriate counter by 1;
        increment the count of integers read so far by 1
    end

The three constructs **begin-end**, **if-then-else**, and **while-do** are used together in an algorithm in accordance with its logic.

The following are two alternative presentations of the algorithm of Example 2–5.

PSEUDOCODE

```
*PROGRAM COUNTS POSITIVE AND NEGATIVE INTEGERS
begin
  Integer N, POSCNT, NEGCNT, I, NUM;
  *INITIALIZE
  Input N;
  POSCNT ← 0; *COUNT OF POSITIVE INTEGERS*
  NEGCNT ← 0; *COUNT OF NEGATIVE INTEGERS*
  I ← 0; *COUNT OF INTEGERS READ IN*
  *COUNT
  while I < N do
    begin
      I ← I + 1;
      Input NUM;
      if NUM ≥ 0 then
        POSCNT ← POSCNT + 1
      else
        NEGCNT ← NEGCNT + 1
    end;
  Output POSCNT, NEGCNT
end
```

FLOWCHART

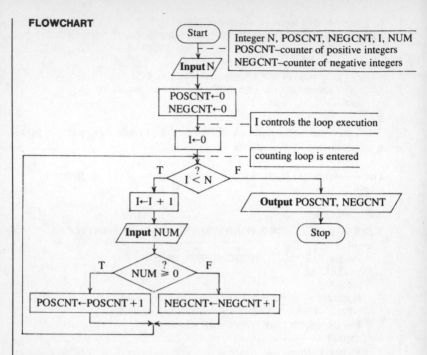

FIGURE 2-7.

In Fig. 2-7 the comments explain the technique; usually they are problem-oriented.

4. ADDITIONAL CONTROL STRUCTURES

To make the programming process easier, additional control structures are used. The following structures are discussed at appropriate points in this book:

repeat-until loop (Chapter 7-F-2);
indexed loop, native to FORTRAN (Chapter 7-E);
case (multiple choice) construct (Chapter 7-G).

In certain cases, when other alternatives are less satisfactory, an unconditional transfer of control (**goto**) may be used. This statement orders the execution of a given statement regardless of its place in the algorithm (or program). The flow of control then proceeds from this statement.

The general form of **goto** statement is

goto label

A *label* is a symbolic address of a program statement. In pseudocode, it is written in front of the statement and often delimited with a special symbol (e.g., a semicolon). As we will see, in FORTRAN all labels are integer numbers.

EXAMPLE 2-6

The following statements may be included in an algorithm:

.
.
.

goto THERE

.
.
.

THERE: SUM ← SMALL + LARGE

.
.
.

When the goto will be executed, control will pass to the statement labeled THERE.

The use of a **goto** should follow a consideration and rejection of other structures for expressing the logic of the program. In many situations, an **exit** statement may be used instead: it transfers control out of a loop to the immediately following statement. This statement, whose use is illustrated in the binary search algorithm presented in Chapter 8-E, makes the reading of the algorithm easier.

In some languages lacking certain control structures, the **goto** statement is used to implement them in a program in a disciplined fashion. FORTRAN is one of these languages. This does not, of course, influence the presentation of algorithms in terms of these structures.

D. EXAMPLE OF AN ALGORITHM

A relatively simple algorithm is presented here in some detail. Many others are discussed in later chapters.

EXAMPLE 2-7. EUCLID'S ALGORITHM

Problem

The greatest common divisor (GCD) of two positive integers is to be determined. (The GCD of two integers is the largest integer by which both of them can be divided exactly.)

Solution

The initial, verbal, solution is subsequently presented in a flowchart form, as well as in the alternative, pseudocode, form.

Solution: Verbal Description of the Algorithm

The larger integer is divided by the smaller one. If the remainder is 0, the smaller integer is the required result; otherwise the larger integer is discarded and the smaller integer is treated as the larger one and the remainder as the smaller one, whereupon the procedure is repeated from the beginning.

Test

The algorithm is checked for the integers 12 and 46.

46 : 12 = 3, remainder = 10
12 : 10 = 1, remainder = 2
10 : 2 = 5, remainder = 0
  GCD = 2

SOLUTION: INITIAL FLOWCHART OF THE ALGORITHM (FIG. 2–8)

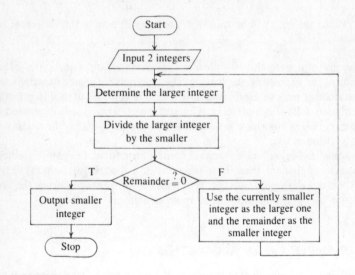

FIGURE 2–8.

SOLUTION: REFINED FLOWCHART (FIG. 2-9)

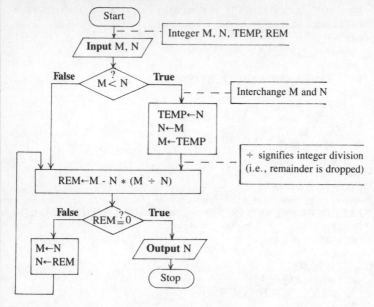

FIGURE 2-9.

SOLUTION: PSEUDOCODE OF THE ALGORITHM

```
*EUCLID'S ALGORITHM FOR FINDING GCD OF TWO POSITIVE
*INTEGERS M AND N
begin
  Integer M, N, TEMP, REM;
  Input M, N;
*DETERMINE THE LARGER INTEGER
  if M < N then
    begin
      TEMP ← N;
      N ← M;
      M ← TEMP
    end
  else;
*COMPUTE REMAINDER
  REM ← M - N * (M ÷ N);
*KEEP DIVIDING AND INTERCHANGING UNTIL THE REMAINDER
*BECOMES 0
  while REM ≠ 0 do
    begin
      M ← N;
      N ← REM;
      REM ← M - N * (M ÷ N)
    end;
  Output N
end
```

Notes

1. Note that in order for the **while** statement to be executed, variable REM ought to have a value. Thus, it is necessary to repeat the statement computing the remainder.

2. Convince yourself that the algorithm works correctly without the initial interchange of variable values if $M < N$. In this case, the interchange occurs as the first iteration of the loop.

Do you think, however, that the algorithm is easier to understand as presented? Do you think the algorithm takes longer to execute as presented (count the number of tests and the number of assignments that will be performed in both cases)?

3
FORTRAN PROGRAMS

While the essential features of the FORTRAN language are the same in every system, some implementations introduce additional features or choose not to provide certain facilities postulated by the language standard. In the final count, this depends on the software translator, usually a compiler, used by the installation.

The programmer should be familiar with all such limitations as well as with the procedures necessary to submit and run a program. While most systems run FORTRAN programs as batch, some do provide interactive facilities.

It is extremely important to realize that programming involves more than just coding in FORTRAN. Before the actual coding, the programmer should analyze the problem and design the algorithm for its solution. The coded program ought to be checked out before the execution and then systematically tested and debugged with the use of the computer. The final product should be carefully documented.

A FORTRAN program has a fixed form, consisting of an ordered set of statements placed in their lines in a certain fashion, which ought to be strictly followed.

A. FORTRAN LANGUAGE AND ITS IMPLEMENTATION

A higher level language, FORTRAN is basically machine-independent, i.e., the make-up of a program ideally does not depend on the computer used to run it.

As described in the Preface, the new FORTRAN standard, FORTRAN 77, coexists at this time with the old one, on which FORTRAN IV is based. A program written in conformance with the old standard will run correctly under the new one (but not the other way around). It is one of the purposes of this book to make it possible for you to write a program conforming to either standard.

It is suggested that you avoid using nonstandard (implementation-dependent) features of the language unless important considerations prevail. A standard program is portable and more readable.

We have already seen in Chapter 1–D that FORTRAN programs are usually translated by compilers. The fate of a FORTRAN program in a computer system is presented in Fig. 3–1 (where the action of the loader, usually transparent to the programmer, is omitted). Since most frequently we submit the program to the computer for the compilation and subsequent execution, the data are presented together with the program.

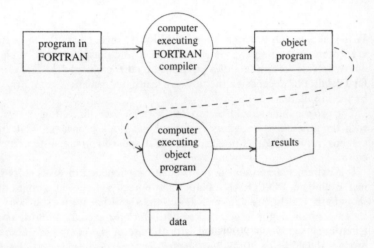

FIGURE 3–1.   Processing of a FORTRAN program

There exist many different FORTRAN compilers. Since standards are voluntary, some of these compilers offer additional features or drop some of the features established by the standard. Thus, if an advanced feature is used, the FORTRAN manual for the given system should be consulted; this is pointed out in certain cases in the text.

Certain compilers, such as WATFOR and WATFIV, are particularly suitable for debugging (rendering programs error-free): they compile quickly and give helpful error messages. They do not produce very efficient machine code, however. At the other end of the compiler spectrum are optimizing compilers: the results of long compilations, they produce very efficient object code. An example is FORTRAN H of the IBM 360–370 systems. Most compilers fall in between these two categories.

Infrequently, FORTRAN is interpreted, i.e., translated and executed statement by statement, without the object program being produced. Such practice (used in time-sharing systems), while convenient to the programmers, results in increased use of computer resources.

When a program is run initially, it often contains *compilation errors* (also known as *syntax errors*): erroneous use of the FORTRAN language itself, discovered by the compiler. (In a time-sharing system, translation errors are indicated by the interpreter.) However, correct compilation does not mean that the program is correct; there may be errors in the algorithm itself leading to incorrect results. (After all, correct use of English does not ensure the soundness of the ideas expressed by the speaker.) The latter, *execution errors,* should be expurgated through systematic testing of the program, as discussed in the next section.

B. HOW TO PROGRAM

Programming is more than simply writing a program. It is rather a task of designing a correct and documented solution to a properly understood problem, then coding this solution as a program and convincing oneself in the correctness of this program. Several stages thus make up the programmer's task. You will do well by systematically carrying out these steps.

(1) Make sure that you are solving the correct problem. Therefore, clearly define and analyze the problem before solving it.

(2) Using pseudocode or flowcharts, design the algorithm of the solution and the data. Several refinements may be needed, depending on the complexity of the problem.

(3) Code a readable program without leaving any details for a later clarification. Using this book (and, if needed, consulting the language manual for your installation), make sure that you are correctly expressing the algorithm in FORTRAN. A program is made readable by:
   • the use of comments to describe the purpose of meaningful sections of code and, in general, to help a reader understand the program
   • the use of meaningful variable names
   • avoiding tricky code (aim for clarity, not for "cleverness" in coding)
   • the use of clear control structures rather than multiple undisciplined **goto**'s
   • indentation of appropriate code segments and spacing
   • keeping to a clear convention in assigning statement labels (numbers).
   This text contains many detailed stylistic remarks, set in boxes. Follow them!

(4) Study and hand-check the program or its crucial fragments. (*Hand-checking* consists in "playing the computer" by simulating the program

execution by hand for a sample input.) Convince yourself also that your program will operate correctly under boundary conditions (e.g., if an input may range between -10 and 10, make sure that the program works for these two values) and in special cases (e.g., that a division by 0 is avoided).

(5) Try to run the program with sample input data and remove any compilation (syntax) errors.

Your compiler will generate diagnostic messages. Due to the nature of the compilation process (and, unfortunately, sometimes, to lack of care on the part of compiler writers), a single error may generate multiple and/or misleading messages. Identify the crucial ones and, with the use of this text and, possibly, a FORTRAN manual for your installation, correct the offending statement(s). Remember that the computer is unforgiving: you cannot take liberties with even a comma.

The process of finding and correcting errors (bugs) is called *debugging*.

(6) When no compilation errors are present, the program may actually be executed. Now it should be tested to demonstrate that it operates correctly. You will need to submit the input data in the allowed range (again, watch for the boundary conditions) and convince yourself that they are processed correctly.

For testing purposes, your program should echo (print out and identify) all the inputs. This provides *echo check* in testing: in beginners' programs inputs are often read in incorrectly. Input values so displayed will also be a part of the documentation.

In most "real-world" programs it is also required that the program reject (print out an appropriate message and stop) any inputs outside the range defined in the problem.

The debugging process is continued to remove execution errors. The essential means of debugging is again hand checking. When a bug is discovered (through an error message or an incorrect result), you will have to work backward through the program to find its source. You will sometimes need temporarily to insert additional statements; usually these are output statements needed to print out certain values and messages that will help you to locate the source of the error. Be careful in correcting errors! Otherwise, compilation errors may appear again.

If your installation provides special software tools for debugging (such as debuggers or traces), by all means use them.

(7) The programmer's task is completed only when the basic documentation is provided along with the successful run. The necessary documentation includes:

- the algorithm expressed as pseudocode or flowchart (usually the last refinement suffices)

- an appropriately commented program with a set of header comments that identify the program, name the author and state the date of completion, explain what the program does, possibly, very briefly state the algorithm or method employed, and explain the purpose of major variables
- a set of sample inputs with their corresponding outputs.

C. HOW TO RUN A PROGRAM

To run a program, a user is required to follow certain procedures. While the essence of these is similar in all systems of a given type (batch or time-sharing), the details are specific to the installation and should be observed scrupulously.

A program, together with the appropriate control information, when submitted to the system is called a job.

FORTRAN programs are most often run in a batch environment, where the job is presented by the user together with the complete data required. After a certain interval, called *turnaround time* (on the order of minutes or hours, depending on the installation), the user obtains full results of the run. If changes are required, the user has to resubmit the job.

In some computer systems, an interactive environment is established via *time-sharing,* a system in which a number of users have access to the computer at the same time. The user then stays at the input/output terminal while the program is being run, presents the data as requested by the program, and is able to make changes in the program on line, interacting with the computer, as it were.

1. IN A BATCH SYSTEM

FORTRAN jobs are most frequently run in a noninteractive environment: the program together with the requisite data are submitted as a card deck or presented in the same form through a terminal.

To run a FORTRAN program, a computer system requires certain information from the programmer in the form of control cards. Although they depend on the installation, they have the following general sequence:

—ID control card: identifies the job and the user
—Control cards to request the use of the FORTRAN compiler and, possibly, other system resources

Program statements

—Control card(s) that delimits the
program from the data

> present only if
> the program
> needs to be
> supplied with data

Data

—End-of-job control card

The exact format of control cards for the specific installation should be obtained. Special cards may have to be included to request certain nonstandard facilities, like punching of the object deck (i.e. the compiled program), etc.

Most systems permit the user to save the program in the form of a file and subsequently recall it from the secondary memory (e.g., a disk) where it is stored.

2. IN A TIME-SHARING SYSTEM

In some installations, FORTRAN jobs are run in a time-sharing environment from a terminal. The following procedure is then followed:

(1) The user "logs onto the system" by presenting an ID number and password (the exact procedure depends on the installation).

(2) The user specifies that the program that follows is in FORTRAN.

(3) The FORTRAN program is entered: Each program line must have a sequence number (not related to any FORTRAN statement numbers). Each consecutive line is to be assigned a higher number, with the numbers reasonably spaced out (e.g., 10, 20, 30) to allow for a possible insertion of additional lines at a later time. At least one blank is to separate the identifying number from the rest of the line, e.g.,

```
100     25 FORMAT(1X, I2)
```

Here 100 is the sequence number and 25 is the statement number (label).

(4) The user orders the program to be run.

(5) According to the input (READ) statements in the program, the system requests the data from the user by printing (or displaying) a question mark. The user then presents the requisite data via the terminal.

Since it is difficult to remember, in general, which data have to be presented at a given stage, it is a good practice to incorporate into the program short messages requesting specific data.

According to the output (PRINT or WRITE) statements in the program, the system prints (or displays) the results and messages to the user.

(6) If errors are detected, correction can be made by referring to the sequence number of the program line. Thus, a line may be deleted or replaced, or a line with a new number may be inserted. The insertion is done automatically according to the sequence number specified by the programmer. Editing facilities are usually available to modify the program.

(7) The program may be saved in the secondary memory as a file with a name assigned by the programmer. Subsequently, recalling the file by its name will be sufficient to run this program.

Every time-sharing system has a set of *commands,* to be employed by the user in order to perform a specific task, such as to store the program in the file library or to run the program. These should be studied and used with care and precision.

D. COMPONENTS OF A FORTRAN PROGRAM

A FORTRAN program consists of statements valid in that language and comments that explain the program without affecting its execution.

As further discussed in Chapter 8, FORTRAN statements may be grouped into independent *program units:* the main program and, if needed, a number of subprograms. We will further assume, until Chapter 8, that when we talk about a program, we mean the main program, which is the necessary part of it.

FORTRAN statements are also classified either executable or nonexecutable. *Executable statements* specify actions to be taken by the machine during the program execution; these are the assignment and input/output statements and the statements that control the flow of execution. *Nonexecutable statements* provide the information to the software translator (usually a compiler) or describe the format of data for input/output (FORMAT statements).

Certain nonexecutable statements (for example, type specifications) are constrained to appear before all executable statements in a program unit.

Program statements and comments have the composition corresponding to an 80-column punched card, the traditional input medium (see Fig. 3–2). This composition holds regardless of the actual medium used (e.g., a display terminal or papertape equipment).

A statement is placed into an 80-column line as follows:

columns 1–5: hold a label, if the statement has one; otherwise left blank. The program is easier to read if the labels are right-justified;

column 6: blank, unless this is a continuation line; such lines are used if a statement does not fit into a single line, or in order to make the program more readable. Any character may indicate a continuation line (e.g., + or $).

columns 7–72: the statement itself;

columns 73–80: usually left blank; the content of these columns, if any, has no influence on the program execution. They may be used to identify certain statements for the programmer's purposes.

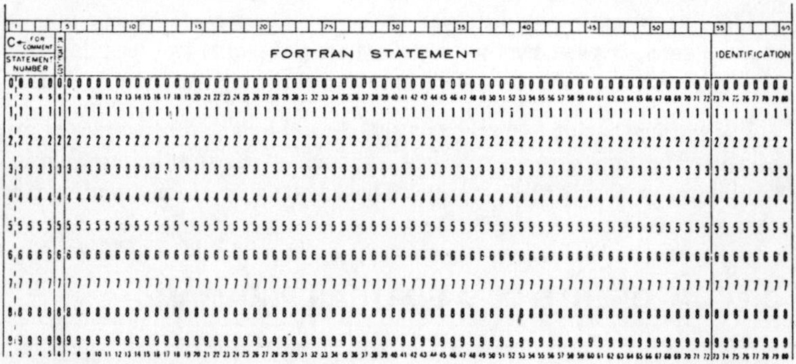

FIGURE 3–2. FORTRAN punched card

To be able to refer to a statement from another one, statement labels are used. A FORTRAN *label* (also called a *statement number*) is a positive integer of one to five digits (unique within a program unit). Labels are appended to executable statements, in order to direct the flow of control in the program, and to FORMAT statements. Thus, only some statements in a program are labeled.

It is advisable that the programmer maintain a consistent method of assigning labels in the program. The numbers should increase down the program unit, with spacing out for insertions. A frequently used convention is to assign a sequence of labels 10, 20, 30, etc., to executable statements and a sequence of high numbers (such as, for example, 501, ..., 509, 511, ...) to FORMAT statements.

A *continuation line,* identified with any symbol other than the blank in column 6, provides for statements longer than 66 characters (columns 7–72). A single statement may be continued on up to 19 such lines.

Blanks may be used freely in a FORTRAN statement (i.e., in columns 7–72) to improve its readability. In particular, they are used to indent certain groups of statements to show the logic of the program.

A *comment* line is identified as follows:

(1) there is a character C in column 1 (the only admissible way in FOR-
  TRAN IV);

▷ (2) an asterisk (∗) appears in column 1;   ◁
(3) the line is blank (i.e., its columns 1–72 are blanks).

The length of a comment line is 72 characters; to extend it, another comment line is appended.

Comment lines may appear anywhere in the program; they are only printed or displayed, without influencing the execution.

> The use of comments is one of the most important documentation techniques
> and should never be neglected.

Data, to be placed appropriately in the job sequence (see Section C–1),
may appear anywhere in columns 1–80 of a line, in correspondence with the
FORMAT statement that serves to read them in, or with the conventions of
format-free input.

The make-up of a very simple FORTRAN program is shown in Fig. 3–3.
A special FORTRAN coding form has been used for the purpose.

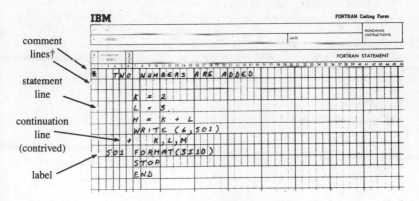

†These methods are valid in FORTRAN 77 only; in FORTRAN IV both lines must start with C.

FIGURE 3–3. A FORTRAN program (shown in a portion of a coding form)

Only the following characters may appear in a FORTRAN program except as character data, to be discussed in Chapter 9, (they are said to constitute the FORTRAN character set):

(1) Alphanumeric characters: capital letters A–Z and digits 0–9;
(2) Special characters shown in Table 3–1.

TABLE 3–1. FORTRAN special characters

CHARACTER	NAME OF CHARACTER	CHARACTER	NAME OF CHARACTER
	blank	)	right parenthesis
=	equals	,	comma
+	plus	.	decimal point
−	minus	$	currency symbol
*	asterisk		
/	slash	'	apostrophe
(	left parenthesis		(single quote)
		:	colon

Most FORTRAN statements are identified by special words, such as READ, WRITE, DO, etc., called *keywords*. Keywords are fixed for the language. A programmer needs, however, to create names for variables, arrays, subroutines, etc. These are called *symbolic names*.

The rules for forming a symbolic name (e.g., a variable name) in FORTRAN are the following:

(1) No more than six characters (but as few as one) are allowed.
(2) First character must be a letter.
(3) Only alphanumeric characters are allowed (i.e., only letters and digits).
(4) In FORTRAN 77, any character other than the first may be a blank.
(5) Names, as much as possible, should describe the entity named.

EXAMPLE 3–1

These are valid symbolic names:

ITEM1, MULT, Z109, X

The following character sequences cannot be used as symbolic names in FORTRAN:

1XYZ

(the first character is a digit)

MULTIPLICAND

(too long)

CASH$

(contains a special character)

4

PROCESSING OF
NUMERICAL DATA. ESSENTIALS

Numerical (also called arithmetic) data are represented in FORTRAN by two essential data types: integer and real. Two other types of arithmetic data—double precision and complex (available only in the full language)—are used in specialized applications.

Along with the arithmetic data, a FORTRAN program may use logical and character data types (character constants are available as a data type only in FORTRAN 77); their manipulation is discussed in Chapter 9.

The manipulation and simplified input/output of integer and real variables are discussed in this chapter. The discussion thus encompasses the following FORTRAN features: numerical type statements, arithmetic expressions and assignment statement, list-directed input/output and elementary formatted input/output, and the make-up of a simple FORTRAN program.

The processing of numerical data is discussed further in Chapter 6; discussion of formatted input/output occurs in Chapter 5.

Meaningful programs are almost always built with the repetitive use of a number of their statements. Such programs must include statements that control the flow of program execution; these are described in Chapter 7.

A. INTEGER AND REAL CONSTANTS

A constant is a value that does not change during the program execution. The two essential types of arithmetic constants in FORTRAN are integers and real numbers. These are also the values assumed by the two essential types of FORTRAN variables.

Data items of the integer type, which are whole numbers, are used to represent entities that cannot have fractional values.

EXAMPLE 4–1
To represent a Social Security number or the number of entries in a table an integer constant is used.

Real values, which may have fractional parts, are generally useful in a computation. Real constants must have decimal points (even though there may be no fractions), integers may not have them. Thus the two are distinguished. The plus sign is optional for positive constants.

EXAMPLE 4-2

5, −153, 0 are integer constants;
5., −153.12, 0. are real constants.

Integer and real values (of constants or variables) are represented differently in computers. The representation of an integer number is always exact; a real value is only (very closely) approximated.

The range of both integer and real values is limited for a given computer system. Real numbers have a much wider range than integers. If large numbers have to be represented, the actual limits for the machine should be ascertained; large numbers can almost always be accommodated as real values.

EXAMPLE 4-3

Most minicomputers can represent integers between −32,767 and 32,767, while the magnitude of representable real numbers ranges approximately from -10^{38} to 10^{38}.

In a real value, the number of significant digits (that is, other than trailing 0's or leading 0's in a pure fraction) is also limited; all machines allow, however, for up to seven digits. This limitation sets a bound on the precision of a number. If greater precision than that afforded with the use of real values is required, a double precision data type should be used (see Chapter 6–E).

To represent a very small or a very large real number concisely, exponential (or scientific) notation may be used instead of the positional one. In such a representation, the exponent specifies the position of the decimal point, and the mantissa specifies the digits of the number; for example here 0.155 is the mantissa and 5 and −2 are exponents:

$$15500 = 0.155 \times 10^5$$
$$-0.00155 = -0.155 \times 10^{-2}$$

In FORTRAN, × 10 is replaced by E, and the exponent is written in line as a signed integer. The above constants are therefore represented as:

0.155E5	and	−0.155E−2
or .155E5	and	−.155E−2

It is convenient to write such constants in the normalized form, with the first significant digit immediately to the right of the decimal point (as shown above). The properties of integer and real constants are summarized in Table 4–1.

TABLE 4–1.

INTEGER AND REAL CONSTANTS (plus sign optional for positive constants)	
integer constant	real constant
no decimal point within the range allowed by the computer (usually at least four or five digits)	always contains a decimal point within the range allowed by the computer (very few problems exceed it) usually at least seven digits of precision scientific notation may be used, with E followed by a signed integer representing the exponent

The following example illustrates the use of these constants:

EXAMPLE 4–4

valid integer constants: +7, 7, −7
valid real constants: 1.137, −55E+3, .55E−03
invalid constants: 5,371, .51E
invalid as real constant: 17
invalid as integer constant: 5.1
probably invalid constants (limits of representation for your computer have to be ascertained): 53712345711, 0.12E+99

B. VARIABLES

A programmer may assign a symbolic name to a memory location. Such a location may then contain any value, unknown to the programmer before the program execution begins and possibly varying during execution. The value may be referred to simply by the name of the memory location that holds it. For example, instead of saying, "multiply the given value by 2," we are able to say, "multiply whatever is in such-and-such location by 2." Thus, we do not have to know the actual value!

Such an entity, with a value, a name, and of a definite type (for example, integer) is called a *variable*. By defining and using variables, the programmer can write programs in which the values of data items are not known before the execution. This actually distinguishes programming from calculation.

Variable names are formed as any other symbolic names in FORTRAN according to the rules specified on p. 34. Therefore, such names as INCOME, PERCNT, or X1 are legal variable names, while 1Y, MARRIED, 007, and X*Y are not.

No two variables in the same program unit (for example, in the main program) may have the same name.

Since the representations in memory of integer and real values differ, the programmer must specify the type of the variable. In FORTRAN, such specification may be accomplished implicitly or explicitly.

1. EXPLICIT SPECIFICATION

A *type statement* is used to specify the type of variables listed in it. The general form of type statements for integer and real variables† is

INTEGER variable name, . . . , variable name
REAL variable name, . . . , variable name

EXAMPLE 4–5

Examples of integer and real type statements are, respectively,

    INTEGER STATE, COUNT, ZIP
    REAL LBS, PRESS

Type statements are nonexecutable. They request that the computer allocate memory locations to store the values of the variables and assign names to these locations. Such statements, which describe data, are often called *declarations*. Type statements should precede all executable statements in a program unit.

2. IMPLICIT SPECIFICATION

A variable name starting with the letters I through N, *unless specified otherwise by a type declaration,* refers to an integer variable. Likewise, a variable name starting with A through H or with O through Z refers to a real variable, unless overridden by explicit declaration.

This naming scheme may be changed with the use of the IMPLICIT statement, usually employed in the following general form:

IMPLICIT INTEGER (character-1–character-2)
IMPLICIT REAL (character-1–character-2)

This signifies that all variable names starting with one of the characters between character-1 and character-2 in the alphabetical sequence are of the type specified. This statement is to be placed before all the type specifications and executable statements in the given program unit.

---

†As will be seen in later chapters, array and function names may also be included.

EXAMPLE 4-6

(a) IMPLICIT REAL (A–Z)
specifies that all program variables are real,
(b) IMPLICIT INTEGER (A–P)
means that variables with names such as ANSWER, COUNT, LENGTH, PRESS are of integer type in this program unit.

> In general, use the IMPLICIT statement only when *all* the variables in a program are to be of a given type [as in Example 4–6(a)].

The alternative ways to specify variable types may be summarized as follows:

(1) with an explicit declaration of type, placed before executable statements;
(2) with an IMPLICIT statement, declaring that the variables whose names start with given letters are of the given type;
(3) by starting the variable name with letters I through N for integer variables and with other letters for real variables.

Remember that a type declaration overrides the type implicitly specified by the starting letter of a variable name.

> In specifying variables advantage should be taken of the full possible length of variable names (six characters). Thus, do not call the variable W, but WEIGHT, if this is what it stands for, so that the name as closely as possible describes the entity represented.
>
> It is advisable to use explicit statements of type for all variables in the program. This helps to avoid conflicts between the meaningful and implicit naming of variables and aids in reliable programming.

A variable has no value until one has been assigned to it either through initialization or as the result of the execution of an assignment or an input statement.

C. ARITHMETIC ASSIGNMENT STATEMENTS

Arithmetic calculations are performed by means of arithmetic assignment statements. Such statements cause an expression to be evaluated and the result to be assigned to a variable (or an array element, as will be seen later).

The order of the evaluation of an expression is determined by the relative precedence of its operands and by the use of parentheses.

While it is preferable to use expressions consisting entirely of integers or of real constants and/or variables, FORTRAN 77 and many variations of FORTRAN IV allow the programmer to employ also mixed-mode expressions that include both of these.

1. GENERAL FORM

An arithmetic assignment statement, used to perform arithmetic in FORTRAN, has the following general form:

variable = arithmetic expression

Thus, an assignment statement assigns a value to a variable (or, as will become clear in Chapter 6, to an array element).

An arithmetic expression consists of one or more arithmetic constants and/or variable names joined pairwise by arithmetic operators. (As will be seen in Chapter 6, an array element may stand in place of a variable name.) Parentheses may be used to impose precedence of evaluation. An arithmetic expression is written like a formula of ordinary algebra.

It is crucial to appreciate that an equal (=) sign denotes an assignment (expressed in algorithmic notation as ←) rather than equality.

EXAMPLE 4–7

Statement

I = I + 1

is meaningful and causes the value of the variable I to be incremented by 1.

During the execution of an assignment statement the following sequence of events occurs:

(1) The arithmetic expression is evaluated according to the rules of precedence (explained below).
(2) The value obtained is assigned to the variable whose name appears on the left-hand side of the assignment statement (i.e., placed in the memory location corresponding to this name).

Values of variables referenced only by the right-hand side of the assignment statement remain unchanged; the previous value of the variable on the left-hand side is replaced by the new one.

EXAMPLE 4–8

These are some encodings of algebraic formulas as FORTRAN assignment statements:

ALGEBRAIC NOTATION	FORTRAN
$x = \dfrac{a + b}{c + d}$	$X = (A + B)/(C + D)$
$x = \dfrac{a + b}{c} + d$	$X = (A + B)/C + D$
$x = abc^d$	$X = A * B * C ** D$

2. ORDER OF EVALUATION OF ARITHMETIC EXPRESSIONS

The order in which an expression is evaluated is determined by the relative precedence of the operators that appear in it, unless superseded by the use of parentheses—similar to the usage in algebra.

Five operations may be specified in a FORTRAN arithmetic expression. These are, with their corresponding operators, addition (+), subtraction (−), multiplication (*), division (/), and exponentiation (**). Only round parentheses may be used.

All operators have to be explicitly placed in the expression. No two operators may appear next to each other.

EXAMPLE 4-9

An algebraic equation

$$y = 2x^3 - 5z + \frac{x}{x + z}\left[x - z(7 - x)\right]$$

is expressed in FORTRAN as

Y = 2 * X ** 3 − 5 * Z + X * (X − Z *(7 − X))/(X + Z)

provided that X, Y, Z are program variables of an arithmetic type.

The usual algebraic order of precedence applies among the operators:

**	highest precedence
* and /	↓
+ and −	lowest precedence

EXAMPLE 4-10

The expression

$$X - Y ** V/W * Z$$

is evaluated in the order

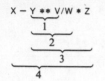

In order to change this order of evaluation, parentheses are used. Parentheses should be matched; i.e., every left parentheses should have a corresponding right parenthesis.

The overall order of expression evaluation is defined by the following rules:

(1) If parentheses are present, the contents of the innermost parentheses are evaluated first. Then the contents of the next enclosing parentheses are evaluated, and so on.

(2) If there are no parentheses, or within a matched pair of parentheses, the operations are performed in the following order of precedence:
> exponentiation;
> multiplication and division;
> addition and subtraction.

(3) Operations of the same level of precedence are performed from left to right.

Blanks may be freely used to increase readability of an assignment statement.

A special consideration is that if two exponentiations follow one another in an expression, parentheses are necessary to define the order of evaluation. This means that to encode

$$(x^y)^z$$

we use

$$(X**Y)**Z$$

and to express

$$x^{(y^z)}$$

we use

X**(Y**Z)

Since two operators may not abut, to encode
$$\frac{x - z}{- y}$$
we use

(X − Z)/(−Y)

EXAMPLE 4–11

It is convenient to represent the order of expression evaluation as a tree. Thus, the order of evaluation of the right-hand side in the assignment statement below is

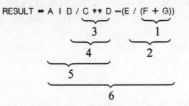

This order of evaluation may be represented by the tree in Fig. 4–1.

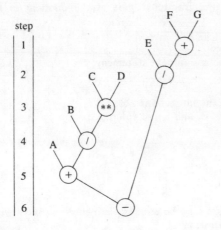

step		
1		currently innermost parentheses
2		currently innermost parentheses
3		operator of highest precedence
4		operator of highest precedence
5		left-to-right rule
6		no other operators

FIGURE 4–1.

This advice will help in your coding:

(1) When in doubt, use parentheses.

(2) If a complex arithmetic expression has to be coded, breaking it up into several assignment statements may increase the readability of your program.

(3) In order to improve readability, you may surround every operator with a blank on each side.

3. TYPE OF ARITHMETIC EXPRESSION

The type of an arithmetic expression is determined by the type of constants and variables that appear in it. If an expression contains constants or variables of a single type, it will be evaluated to a result of this type. In a mixed-mode expression containing both integer and real data types, integer operands are automatically converted to the real form and the result is a real number. The use of mixed-mode expressions often leads to effects unexpected by the programmer and should therefore be avoided.

A. INTEGER ARITHMETIC

If an expression contains only integer constants and variables, integer arithmetic is used to evaluate it. In integer arithmetic *integer division* (division of two integer values) yields an integer value also. This occurs as the result of automatic *truncation:* the fractional part of the quotient is simply dropped.

EXAMPLE 4–12

(a) The execution of the assignment statement

$I = 5/2$

yields 2 as the value of the integer variable I.

(b) If K has the value of 3, and L the value of 5, then

$M = K/L$

yields M having the value 0.

EXAMPLE 4–13

Note that integer division may be used to distinguish between even and odd integers. If the expression

$(K / 2) * 2$

evaluates to the value of K, then the value of K is even; otherwise, it is odd.

B. REAL ARITHMETIC

If an expression contains only real constants and variables, real arithmetic is used to evaluate it.

Since the representation of a real number in the computer memory has only finite precision, the results of real arithmetic are not entirely exact. Although in an overwhelming majority of programming situations, the programmer does not have to consider this fact, one should be aware of this limitation, and act accordingly:

- Do not count with real variables instead of integers.
- Do not test for equality of real values, some of which are obtained through a computation, since 10./100. in computer arithmetic may not equal 0.1: Although it may be so printed, it may actually equal 0.0999. . . .

▷ C. MIXED-MODE EXPRESSIONS

Mixed-mode expressions contain both integer and real constants and/or variables. While not allowed by the "old" FORTRAN standard, these have been permitted by many compilers and are allowed by FORTRAN 77.

A mixed-mode expression with integer and real values is evaluated according to the general rules of precedence. In any arithmetic operation in which one operand is integer and the other real, the integer is converted to the real number representation. (This does not change the value of the number itself but may affect the result.) Real arithmetic is then used.

The exception is exponentiation: an integer operand used to raise a real value to an integer power is not converted.

EXAMPLE 4-14

If the values of the integer variables are

I = 2   J = 5,

while the value of a real variable is

R = 5.0

the following expression

I/J * R

evaluated, naturally, from left to right yields

2/5 * 5. = 0 * 5. = 0. * 5. = 0.

Note the sequence of conversions in this example. This final result will seldom be intended, and the mistake may be difficult to find in a complicated expression.

Note that if the order of the operands is different, namely,

R * I/J

we obtain

5. * 2/5 = 5. * 2./5 = 10./5 = 10./5. = 2.

which is what one would expect. (Some of the steps shown above indicate a conversion from integer to real representation.)

The use of mixed-mode expressions may bring results not expected by the programmer and should be avoided. If the programmer desires to convert an integer value to a real one, it should be done explicitly with the use of the intrinsic function FLOAT (see Chapter 6–C).

---

4. ASSIGNMENT STATEMENTS WITH TWO SIDES OF DIFFERENT TYPES

If the assignment statement has the following form

integer variable = real expression

or   integer variable = mixed-mode (integer and real) expression

the sequence of events is

(1) The expression is evaluated and a real value is obtained.
(2) *This result is truncated* (i.e., its fractional part, if any, is dropped) and assigned to the integer variable.

If the assignment statement has the form:

real variable = integer expression

then:

(1) The expression is evaluated with the use of integer arithmetic.
(2) The representation of the result is converted to the representation of a real number, *without change in value,* and assigned to the real variable.

EXAMPLE 4–15

(a) If I is an integer variable, the statement

I = 2.5

assigns the value 2 to I due to truncation.

(b) Assume I and J are integer variables while A is real. If

    I = 2, J = 3

then

    A = I/J   results in A = 0.
    A = J/I   results in A = 1.

(due to integer division).

This form of implicit conversion between variable types should be avoided in favor of explicit type conversion via intrinsic functions FLOAT and IFIX (see Chapter 6–C).

---

5. SUMMARY OF ASSIGNMENT RULES

The most important FORTRAN rules concerning arithmetic assignment statement are these:

(1) The value of the variable on the left-hand side is replaced by the value of the expression.
(2) An expression is evaluated in the order dictated by parentheses, operator precedence, and the left-to-right rule.
(3) If a real value is being assigned to an integer variable, the fractional part of this value is dropped.
(4) The result of the division of two integers is truncated.
(5) Mixed-mode expressions are to be avoided; in such expressions integer values are converted to the real form.
(6) Blanks may be used between operators and operands to increase readability.

D. SIMPLE INPUT/OUTPUT

To input program data, a FORTRAN programmer most frequently uses punched cards or a terminal keyboard. The output is presented as a printout or on the screen of a display terminal.

The simplest method of reading in the data needed by the program and delivering the program output is the so-called list-directed input/output. This technique does not offer the programmer any control over the layout of data. It is often used in a time-sharing environment, where such layout is difficult to control anyhow and is not important. List-directed input/output is a part of FORTRAN 77; many earlier compilers such as WATFOR and

WATFIV introduced it also (as so-called format-free input/output), even though it was not a part of the old standard.

Complete mastery of input/output is gained by familiarity with formatted input/output, described in the Chapter 5. For the programmers whose systems do not provide list-directed input/output, a serviceable smattering of formatted input/output is presented in this section.

1. LIST-DIRECTED INPUT/OUTPUT (FORTRAN 77)

List-directed input/output provides the simplest method of accessing and delivering data by a program. It is particularly recommended for initial programming work. The method relieves the programmer both of the task of specifying the format of data and of control over its layout. In a time-sharing environment, where such control is most often difficult and unnecessary, this is a frequently used input/output method.

This method, standard in FORTRAN 77, was not a part of the old standard and thus of FORTRAN IV. As *format-free input/output,* it has been, however, widely implemented, in particular, in the popular WATFOR and WATFIV dialects. Before using it, ascertain whether your installation provides this facility.

A. INPUT

The general form of the input statement is

READ *, input list

where "input list" is a list of variable names (as will be discussed in Chapter 6, it also may include array or array element names) separated by commas. For example,

READ *, ITEM, CODE, VALUE1

The essential medium used for such input is a punched card (see Fig. 3–2).

Note that no asterisk (*) is required by the WATFOR and WATFIV compilers.

The values of the variables listed must be presented by the programmer as data in the same order. The type of data must match the type of the variables.

The following rules will guide you in using list-directed input and presenting data:

(1) The data items presented for input should be separated by a comma and/or one or more blanks (spaces).
(2) Integer data may not have decimal points; real data ought to have them. Real numbers may be presented in positional or exponential form (see Chapter 4–A).

(3) Each READ statement reads one card (or one line of data presented through a terminal). After a card has been read, it cannot be read again, "it has been passed." A READ statement "uses up" the card it starts reading. Note that a READ statement without an input list simply causes a card to be skipped.

(4) If there are fewer variables on the input list than data items on the card read, the remaining data will be ignored.

If there are more variables on the input list than there are data items on the card, the next card is read by this READ statement. Further cards will be read until all the variables on the list are assigned values or until there are no more cards (unless an error condition, such as an integer variable being assigned a real value, is detected and the reading stops with an error indication).

EXAMPLE 4-16

Study carefully this "matching" of data with input lists (pitfalls abound).

The following READ statements are executed in this sequence in a program (implicit types are assumed):

```
10 READ *, I, J
20 READ *,
30 READ *, R, M, X
40 READ *, N
```

The following data are supplied:
  card 1: 18, 1743
  card 2: 133
  card 3: 15.5, 23
  card 4: .123E−17, 21, 21
  card 5: 31

The following values are assigned to variables:

STATEMENT EXECUTED	VALUES ASSIGNED	CARDS READ
10	I = 18, J = 1743	1
20	—	2
		The card is skipped—see rule (3).
30	R = 15.5, M = 23	3 and 4
	X = .123E−17	Two last values on card 4 are ignored—see rule (4).
40	N = 31	5

Note that the card 4 has been read by statement 30 in order to complete the assignment of values to its input list and has been "used up" by it without having been fully read.

> To avoid mishaps, place (if possible) on each card only the data needed to satisfy the READ statement that reads it in.

B. OUTPUT

The general form of the list-directed output statement is

$$\text{PRINT } *, \text{ output list}$$

where the output list may contain:

variable names;
array and array element names (to be discussed in Chapter 6);
characters enclosed in single quotes (');
expressions (not in all implementations).

These items are separated by commas or by spaces. Note that no asterisk (*) is required by WATFOR and WATFIV compilers.

EXAMPLE 4-17

The statement

```
PRINT *, 'VALUE = ', RESIST, ' IF LOADED, THEN ', 2.*RESIST
```

will cause the following to be printed if the value of the variable RESIST is 17.34:

```
VALUE = 17.34 IF LOADED, THEN 34.68
```

Here the items are separated by commas.

The exact format of the printout (i.e., the print positions), over which the programmer has no control, depends on the implementation. The following rules apply:

(1) The characters enclosed in quotes will be printed exactly as specified, including blanks.
(2) In every implementation, a fixed number of columns is allocated for the value of each number. Integers are usually printed right-justified in this space. Real numbers will be printed in positional notation, or, if such printing will exceed the space allotted, in exponential notation (see Chapter 4–A).

A number may be automatically rounded off to be fitted into the space allotted.

(3) The order in which the items are printed corresponds to their order on the output list.

The programmer should remember that all the variables whose names appear in the output list ought to have had values assigned to them before the PRINT statement is executed.

2. ELEMENTARY FORMATTED INPUT/OUTPUT

A serviceable, first-care introduction to formatted input/output for numerical computation is offered here. It is sufficient only for a novice programmer. A full discussion of the method is presented in Chapter 5.

To input data the following statement is used:

READ (unit number, FORMAT label) list of variables, separated by commas

where the unit number in the case of a card-reader is 5 in most systems (check this for your system) and the FORMAT label is the statement number of the FORMAT statement that shows the layout of the data. For example,

    READ (5,501) I, J, K

may refer to the FORMAT statement

    501 FORMAT(3I10)

To output data the following statement is used:

WRITE (unit number, FORMAT label) list of variables, separated by commas

where the unit number is 6 in the case of a printer in *most* systems (check!). This statement also always refers to a FORMAT; for example,

    WRITE (6,501) I, J, K

The order of data read or written corresponds to the order of variables in the list. If only integers or real values are to be read/written, the following simple method may be used.

To input or output up to eight integer numbers, punched on a single card or presented on a single line, use

label FORMAT(8I10)

For example, to input three numbers, we could use, instead of the statement 501 above, the following statement:

    501 FORMAT(8I10)

To input up to eight real numbers, use

label FORMAT(8F10.0)

To output up to eight real numbers, use

label FORMAT (8G15.4)

provided that your printed page (or display) is at least 120 columns wide (each number will occupy 15 columns). The numbers will be printed (displayed) in positional notation, unless the number is very small or very large, in which case it will be printed in exponential notation (see Chapter 4–A).

The following apply to this simplified formatted input/output.

(1) You may use the same FORMAT for input and output, if applicable, by referring to its label in a READ and a WRITE statement.

(2) All labels of FORMAT statements in a program should be, of course, distinct. For a numbering convention see Chapter 3–C.

(3) Integer data presented for input must not have decimal points; real numbers ought to have them.

(4) Each integer or real number presented for input is assumed to occupy 10 columns (8 × 10 = 80, the number of card columns). Integer numbers have to be right-justified in their fields (otherwise, the trailing blanks will be considered 0's!). Real numbers may be placed in their 10-column field in any position.

(5) An integer printed with the use of the above numbers occupies 10 columns; a real number, 15 columns.

(6) Every READ statement causes a new card to be read; every WRITE statement causes a new line to be printed (displayed).

(7) Naturally, you may mix the input or output of integers and of real numbers. However, the type of data in the input or output should correspond to the FORMAT specification. To mix the numbers, you simply have to count them and to specify this count in the READ or WRITE statement accordingly, as shown in the example below.

EXAMPLE 4–18

(a) The following statements assign values to the real variables R and V and to the integer variable I in this order:

```
      READ (5,515) R, V, I
 515  FORMAT(2F10.0, I10)
```

This data card is used, where the numbers on top refer to column numbers:

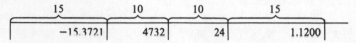

```
    1    5   10    15   20    25   30
              ↓          ↓          ↓
  _____
  /      34.315      −.221      −11

         ‿‿‿‿‿‿‿‿‿   ‿‿‿‿‿‿‿‿‿   ‿‿‿‿‿‿‿‿‿
            10          10          10
```

(b) The statements

```
    WRITE (6,521) Z, K, L, Y
521 FORMAT(G15.4, 2I10, G15.4)
```

will cause the following printout, assuming implicit types of variables and their respective values:

```
       15              10         10            15
     ‿‿‿‿‿‿‿‿‿      ‿‿‿‿‿‿‿     ‿‿‿‿‿‿‿    ‿‿‿‿‿‿‿‿‿‿‿
  |   −15.3721  |    4732  |       24  |    1.1200  |
```

Note that four fractional digits of a real number are printed.

E. MAKE-UP OF A SIMPLE FORTRAN PROGRAM

A FORTRAN program consists of at least one program unit—the main program. (As will be seen in Chapter 8, a program may also include subprograms.)

Program statements are accompanied by control cards, as presented in Chapter 3–C.

The make-up of a program is as follows:

(1) Type statements (e.g., INTEGER or REAL) precede all executable statements.

(2) Executable statements are ordered in accordance with the program logic.

(3) The last two statements in the main program are

STOP—executable statement (it can, therefore, bear a label) which orders the program execution to be halted; and

END—a statement that delimits all others in every program unit.

▷ In FORTRAN 77, it is possible to use as the first statement in the main program the statement

PROGRAM program name

where "program name" is a symbolic name assigned to the entire program. ◁

FORMAT statements may be placed anywhere in the program (following the PROGRAM statement, if it is used).

> As a matter of style, it is suggested that every FORMAT statement be placed immediately after the first READ or WRITE statement that refers to it.

Comments may be placed anywhere in the program. In programs conforming to the old standard, these start with the letter C in column 1.

▷ In FORTRAN 77, comments may start with an asterisk (*), and blank lines may be used to provide readability.   ◁

Every program should contain comments explaining its purpose and logic.
A program should be preceded by a set of comments that constitute its header, as explained in Chapter 3–B.

All major steps in the program should be commented on in the terms of the problem being solved. However, too many comments should be avoided. The criterion is the degree to which the program may be read and understood.

EXAMPLE 4–19

Only a very simple program can be produced without the use of statements that alter the flow of control from sequential execution.

The example below is encoded both according to the old standard and in FORTRAN 77. Note that the first version is correct in both cases but not vice-versa.

PROGRAM PRESENTED IN FORTRAN IV

```
C    PROGRAM: CIRCLE
C    AUTHOR:            DATE:
C
C    CIRCUMFERENCE AND AREA OF A CIRCLE WITH THE GIVEN RADIUS
C                            ARE COMPUTED
C
C    RADIUS - OF THE CIRCLE
C    CIRCUM - CIRCUMFERENCE OF THE CIRCLE
C    AREA   - OF THE CIRCLE
C
     IMPLICIT REAL (A-Z)
     PI = 3.1416
     READ (5,501) RADIUS
501  FORMAT(F10.0)
     CIRCUM = 2. * PI * RADIUS
     AREA = PI * RADIUS ** 2
     WRITE (6,502) RADIUS,CIRCUM,AREA
502  FORMAT(3G15.4)
     STOP
     END
```

A sample output:

```
    5. 3719          33. 7527          90 6581
```

PROGRAM IN FORTRAN 77, WITH LIST-DIRECTED INPUT/OUTPUT

```
      PROGRAM CIRCLE
*    AUTHOR:           DATE:

*    CIRCUMFERENCE AND AREA OF A CIRCLE WITH  THE GIVEN RADIUS
*                          ARE COMPUTED

*    RADIUS - RADIUS OF THE CIRCLE

      IMPLICIT REAL (A-Z)
      PI = 3. 1416
      READ *, RADIUS
*    COMPUTE CIRCUMFERENCE AND AREA
      PRINT *, RADIUS, 2*PI*RADIUS, PI*RADIUS**2
      STOP

      END
```

The same data card may be used for input in both programs. The same output is obtained, but layout depends on the implementation.

5

FORMATTED INPUT/OUTPUT

The formatted method of data input and output consists of accompanying a READ or WRITE statement with a FORMAT statement that specifies the layout of data. As distinguished from list-directed (format-free) input/output, formatting gives the programmer complete control over the layout.

To input data, a FORTRAN programmer most frequently employs punched card equipment or a terminal keyboard; in the latter case the data are made to look the same as they do on a punched card. The output (i.e., results) are presented through a printer or a display. During program execution, all data are assumed to be held in the main memory of the computer.

When an application requires that large collections of data be maintained and processed by the computer system, external files are used. These are stored in secondary memory, i.e., on a tape or on a disk. This mode of data storage is employed chiefly in business data processing. FORTRAN features supporting processing of external files have been significantly expanded in FORTRAN 77. As they are advanced and specialized facilities, they are not discussed in this book.

All the other information necessary for formatted input/output of integer and real data is presented in this chapter.† The input/output of arrays and special types of numerical data is discussed in Chapter 6. The input/output of character and logical data is covered in Chapter 9.

A. CONCEPTS OF FORTRAN INPUT/OUTPUT

Input is used to assign values to variables; the value of constants is stated directly in the program itself. Similarly, the values of variables may be presented on output.††

---

† The details of formatted input/output presented in this chapter may be covered gradually as the reader moves on to the chapters that follow.

†† As will be seen in later chapters, the values of array elements and functions may also be read in or written.

The essential medium for FORTRAN input is a punched card (see Fig. 3–2). Cards used for FORTRAN input data may hold up to 80 alphanumeric characters in their 80 columns. If a terminal keyboard is used for input, the card form is also followed.

The output from a FORTRAN program is mainly obtained on a printer. Usually, line printers have a line width of 132 characters, although narrower printers may be used. If output is displayed on a terminal display, the line width is usually smaller. For all but the simplest of problems, a programmer should ascertain the width of the output available.

A single card of 80 columns (or its corresponding terminal line) is considered a physical record, simply called a *record* (of input). Similarly, a single line of the printer is a single output record.

As will be seen, FORTRAN input/output is designed in terms of reading input records and writing (printing) output records.

There are two essential methods of performing input/output in FORTRAN:

(1) formatted input/output: This, the most frequently used method, gives the programmer control over the layout of data by formulating pairs of statements for every input or output operation: The first of these names the data, and the second specifies the layout (i.e., how the data are to be edited).

▷ (2) list-directed input/output: a simplified method to read or print data, described in Chapter 4. A single statement is used to name the data concerned; the layout is automatic. This method is often used in time-sharing environments, where the layout is difficult to control and is of little interest. It is recommended for a beginning programmer since it avoids the complexities of formatting. ◁

In both cases, the input is performed by a READ statement with its input list, which causes the next record to be accessed and the values in it to be assigned to the entities on the input list.

Output is performed by a WRITE statement in the case of formatted input/output

▷ and by a PRINT statement in list-directed input/output. ◁

These statements cause the values of the entities on the output list to be printed (displayed) beginning with the next record, i.e., on the next line.

Formatted input/output is governed by a nonexecutable FORMAT statement referred to by the executable READ or WRITE statement.

B. READ AND WRITE STATEMENTS

To perform formatted input/output, the programmer has to include:

the input (READ) or the output (WRITE) statement with its input or output list;

a FORMAT statement that describes the layout of data to be read in or written out.

The general format of the input and output statements used most frequently is

READ (unit number, FORMAT label) input list
WRITE (unit number, FORMAT label) output list

where

unit number: specifies the device to be used in the data transfer;

FORMAT label: refers to the FORMAT statement that controls this transfer;

input list: the list of variables (or array and array element names, as discussed in Chapter 6), whose elements are separated by commas;

▷   output list: similar to the input list; however, according to the FORTRAN 77 standard it may also include quoted character strings or expressions, similar to the output list used in list-directed output (see Example 4–17). ◁

In either list, the items are specified in the order they are to be read (written).

Usually, input is performed from the card-reader, a device which in almost all installations has the unit number of 5; output goes to the printer with unit number of 6 (however, make sure this is the case in your installation).

Examples of the above statements are

```
    READ (5,501) I, J, A
    WRITE (6,501) I, J, A
501 FORMAT(2I10, F10.2)
```

The READ statement is executed as follows: The next data record (usually a card) is obtained, and the values presented on it are assigned in sequence to the items on the input list; more than one card may be read to satisfy the list. The cards are read, and the data are interpreted, in accordance with the FORMAT statement referred to.

The WRITE statement is executed as follows: The next record (i.e., line) is begun; if the device is a printer, this and possibly succeeding lines are printed with the values of items on the output list. The layout is in accordance with the FORMAT statement referred to.

C. FORMAT STATEMENT

FORMAT statements describe the form in which data are presented when being read in or, alternatively, when being displayed as output.

These nonexecutable statements may be placed anywhere in the program unit and must have labels so that READ/WRITE statements may refer to them. A single FORMAT may be used (i.e., referred to) by a number of READ and/or WRITE statements.

To make the program easier to read, adopt a standard way of placing and labeling FORMAT's. It is suggested that the FORMAT statement be placed immediately after the first READ or WRITE that refers to it (alternatively, all FORMAT's may be placed at the beginning or at the end of the program).

A convenient convention for the labeling of FORMAT's is the following sequence, starting at the beginning of the program: 501, ..., 509, 511, ...

The general form of FORMAT statement is

label FORMAT (format specification)

For example,

505 FORMAT(2I10, 3F10.2)

The format specification consists of a number of *edit descriptors* that indicate the type and format of particular data items to be read or written, fixed text fragments to be written, and field separators and special symbols that describe the layout of data.

Thus, a record (card or line) is treated as consisting of *fields,* groups of one character columns. The FORMAT statement "edits" data into or from these fields; for this reason edit descriptors are also known as *field descriptors.*

Edit descriptors are separated by commas when only separation is intended. A slash, serving to complete a record (as discussed below) may also serve as a separator.

The next three sections present the most commonly used edit descriptors: I, F, E, and G. These are used for the input and output of integers (I), input and output of real numbers in positional or exponential notation (F, E, or G), and output of real numbers in exponential notation only (E).

D. HOW TO READ AND WRITE INTEGERS

In order to input or output integers, use the edit descriptor of the general form

$$Iw$$

where w specifies the width of the field, i.e., the number of columns in it. If more than one such field is desired in sequence, a repeat specification r may be used as follows:

$$rIw$$

For example,

3I10

1. INPUT

The rules governing the input of integers (Iw) are the following:

(1) An integer constant should have no more than w digits, including the sign if present; it must not contain a decimal point.

(2) Any blanks† within the specified field are interpreted as 0's. Therefore, the number should be right-justified in its field.

(3) Plus signs may be omitted.

> **EXAMPLE 5–1**
>
> (a) A program contains the following statements:
>
>   READ (5,575) LENGTH
>   575 FORMAT(I10)
>
> The integer variable LENGTH is assigned the value contained in the first 10 columns of the next data card. This value is interpreted according to the rules enumerated before this example.
>
> (b) Statements
>
>   READ (5,503) I, J, K
>   503 FORMAT(I10, 2I4)
>
> may be used to read the following card:
>
>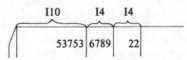
>
> (c) The following table further illustrates the input of integers:

---

† We will use □ to represent a blank in this chapter.

APPEARANCE OF THE FIELD ON THE CARD	EDIT DESCRIPTOR	INTERNAL VALUE (IN MEMORY)
57	I2	57
□57	I3	57
−57	I3	−57
57□	I3	570 (probably not intended)

Note that care is needed to have the integer no longer than w and right-justified in its field.

2. OUTPUT

The rules governing the output of integers (Iw) are the following:

(1) Integers are printed (displayed) right-justified in the field of width w.

(2) Only minus signs are printed; positive numbers are printed without signs.

(3) The first character of any line to be printed is used to control the printer carriage (see Section J of this chapter). Thus, this character will not actually be printed.

To start the new line in an ordinary, single-spaced fashion, it is simplest to insert "1X," before other edit descriptors in a FORMAT statement used for output. This causes a blank to be inserted for carriage control, without this blank being printed [see Example 5–2(a)].

The space allotted (i.e., the field width w) should be sufficient to print the integer. If the space is too large, the portion of the field to the left of the number contains blanks. If the space is not sufficient, in most implementations the field is filled with special characters (e.g., * or $).

> The programmer should carefully allot sufficient space; I10 will almost always do.

EXAMPLE 5–2

(a) The following statements:

```
    WRITE (6,531) L, M, N
531 FORMAT(1X, 2I5, I8)
```

will cause this to be printed:

35	137	3456789
I5	I5	I8

(We assume these values of the variables, of course.)
Note the use of the leading 1X descriptor, which specifies the fictitious blank for carriage control.

(b) This table further exemplifies integer output:

INTERNAL VALUE (IN MEMORY)	EDIT DESCRIPTOR	PRINTED FIELD
57	I2	57
−57	I3	−57
−57	I5	□□−57
−57	I2	**

E. HOW TO READ REAL NUMBERS

Three edit descriptors may be used to read in real numbers. Their general form is, respectively:

$$Fw.d, Ew.d, \text{ and } Gw.d$$

where w specifies the total width of the field holding the real number and d specifies the number of digits to the right of the decimal point.

To specify more than one real number in sequence with any of these descriptors, an integer repeat specification r may be used;

$$rFw.d, \quad rEw.d, \quad rGw.d$$

All three descriptors may be used to input a real number represented either in positional or in exponential notation (see Chapter 4–A). Some nonstandard implementations (such as WATFOR and WATFIV, for example) limit the applicability of the F descriptor to the numbers in positional notation, however.

For example, the following numbers may be read in with these descriptors:

$$13.5, \ -1217., \ -1.531E-12, \ 123E5$$

Exponential notation is convenient in the case of very small or very large numbers.

The use of these descriptors for output differs; a descriptor is often selected for input with a view toward using the same FORMAT statement for output.

The rules governing the input of real numbers (F, E, or G mode), e.g., Fw.d, are the following:

(1) If the number itself contains a decimal point, the value of d in the descriptor is ignored. Otherwise, it determines the position of the decimal point. It is more reliable to place the decimal point in the number itself, if possible.

(2) Blanks within the field w are interpreted as 0's.

(3) A number presented in positional notation does not have to be right-justified in its field, since its decimal point or the value of d delimits the decimal point. A number presented in exponential notation has to be right-justified; otherwise the trailing 0's are considered a part of the integer exponent.

(4) In a number presented in exponential notation, the letter E may be omitted from the data, and the sign of the exponent may be used to indicate its position.

(5) In a number shown in exponential notation, if the mantissa contains no decimal point, the value of d determines its position as follows:

  (a) The total value of the number with the consideration of the exponent is determined.

  (b) The decimal point is shifted right or left according to the value of d.

EXAMPLE 5-3

(a) The following statements:

```
    READ (5,535) A, B, C, D
535 FORMAT(2F10.2, E12.4, G14.2)
```

may be used to assign values to the real variables A, B, C, D from the following card:

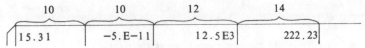

10	10	12	14
15.31	−5.E−11	12.5E3	222.23

Note that since all the fields contain decimal points, the specification of d's in the FORMAT does not influence the interpretation of values on the card. The values are assigned as punched on the card.

(b) Further examples are tabulated below:

APPEARANCE ON THE CARD	EDIT DESCRIPTOR (F, E, OR G)	INTERNAL VALUE (IN MEMORY)
with the decimal point on the card (d is ignored)		
−35.1451	10.2	−35.1451
−3514.51E−2	11.2	−35.1451
□□−3514.51E−2	13.2	−35.1451
□−3514.51E−2□	13.2	-3514.51×10^{-20} (!)
□−3514.51□□E2	13.2	−351451
without decimal point on the card (d determines the position of the decimal point)		
□−351451□□	10.2	−351451
□□□−351451	10.2	−3514.51
□□35145E−1	10.2	35.145

The last result was determined as follows: the value on the card is 35145×10^{-1} = 3514.5; since d = 2, the value stored is $3514.5 \times 10^{-2} = 35.145$. Similarly,

□□□35145E2	10.2	35145

It is recommended that, whenever possible, the decimal point be placed directly in the input data. This makes the data readable on such a medium as a card. The programming is also simplified, since only the field length w has to be precisely stated in the edit descriptor.

F. HOW TO WRITE REAL NUMBERS

The three edit descriptors F, E, G used for input/output of real numbers differ with respect to the form of output they provide.

As with the integer output (see Section E), the first character in a line sent to a line printer should be a carriage control character.

1. OUTPUT IN POSITIONAL NOTATION

To output data in positional notation (without an exponent), an F edit descriptor of the general form

Fw.d

is used; repeat specification may also be used (rFw.d).

Here, w specifies the width of the field in which the number is to be printed (displayed), while d determines the desired number of fractional digits to be printed (displayed).

The rules governing the output of real numbers in positional notation (F descriptor: Fw.d) are the following:

(1) The number is printed (displayed) right-justified in its field w.
(2) In general,

$$w \geqslant d + 3$$

is needed to provide for: the sign (only a minus is printed), 0 (if the number is purely fractional), and the decimal point.

(3) If the number of fractional digits in the number to be printed is larger than d, then the number is *rounded* to the least significant digit as specified by d. Thus, d determines the precision of the number.

(4) If w is not sufficient, the number cannot be printed, and in most implementations a special symbol (* or $, for example) is substituted for it.

When the unknown magnitude of the real number may be large and it is inconvenient to provide for it with the F edit descriptor, E or G descriptors should be used, as described in Sections F–2 and F–3.

EXAMPLE 5–4

(a) The following statements:

```
    WRITE (6,525) X, Y
525 FORMAT(1X, 2F10.2)
```

cause, with the appropriate values of the variables, this printout:

-34.25	-0.13
10	10

(b) This table further exemplifies the output with an F edit descriptor.

INTERNAL VALUE (IN MEMORY)	EDIT DESCRIPTOR	PRINTED FIELD	COMMENTS
-33.241	F8.3	□-33.241	
-33.241	F8.1	□□□-33.2	round-off
-33.241	F6.3	******	7 columns needed
$-33.$	F8.1	□□□-33.0	
$-.1$	F8.1	□□□□-0.1	

Naturally, edit descriptors for integer and real constants may be used in the same FORMAT statement to match the type of variables in the input/output lists, as shown in the following example.

EXAMPLE 5-5

In the following statements, assume implicit variable types:

```
    READ (5,515) I, A, J, X, Y
515 FORMAT(I3, F10.2, I11, 2F7.2)
```

The following values will be correctly read in:

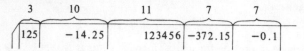

2. OUTPUT IN EXPONENTIAL NOTATION

To output very large or very small real numbers, exponential notation (see Chapter 4–A) is desirable. It permits the placing of the number in a shorter field in a standard (normalized) form.

In order to print a number in exponential notation, the E edit descriptor of the general form

$$Ew.d$$

is utilized.

The rules for the output of real numbers in exponential notation (Ew.d) are the following:

(1) The number is printed (displayed) right-justified in its field.
(2) The number is printed in the following form:

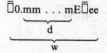

Thus the mantissa of the number is always a fraction with the first significant digit different from 0 (i.e., the number is normalized). Only minus signs are printed; otherwise the sign column is blank (this is shown as ⬚).

(3) As in the case of the F descriptor, the number may be rounded off to the least significant digit of the mantissa as specified by d.

(4) Note that, in general, we should have

$$w \geq d + 7$$

which may be concluded from the printed form of the number shown in (2) above.

EXAMPLE 5-6

(a) The following statements:

```
      WRITE (6,571) X, Y
  571 FORMAT(1X, 2E10.3)
```

cause the printout below:

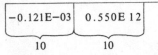

(b) The output in exponential notation is further exemplified by the following table:

INTERNAL VALUE (IN MEMORY)	EDIT DESCRIPTOR	PRINTED FIELD
−33.241	E12.5	−0.33241E 02
−33.2	E12.5	−0.33200E 02
−33.241	E12.3	☐☐−0.332E 02 (note round-off)
.0051	E12.2	☐☐☐☐0.51E−02

3. FLEXIBLE OUTPUT (G EDIT DESCRIPTOR)

The F editing mode is, in general, the simplest to use and renders an output that is easiest to interpret. It is, however, awkward to use when the output of very small or very large unknown values is required. In this latter case we recommend the E mode for providing output in exponential form.

The G edit descriptor is used when the values that may be assumed by the variable to be printed out are not known when the program is being written, but are expected to be such that in the majority of cases they may be output in the preferable F mode, with the exception of some cases when the E mode may be required.

The general form of the G edit descriptor is

$$Gw.d$$

On input, the G descriptor works precisely as the F descriptor would (see Section E above), reading in real numbers in both the positional and exponential notations.

On output, it presents numbers that are "not too small and not too large" (the precise delimitation is outside of our scope here) the way an F descriptor would; otherwise, it acts as E descriptor.

The use of the G mode is similar to the use of the E mode (on output, we need $w \geq d + 7$).

G. HOW TO LEAVE BLANK SPACES

In order to skip n spaces (for example, to leave blank spaces on a printed line or to skip spaces on a card being read in), an X edit descriptor of the general form

$$nX$$

is used.

EXAMPLE 5-7

(a) We use the 1X descriptor to provide for one space at the beginning of every line for carriage control (see Section J below), e.g.,

```
    WRITE (6,514) K
514 FORMAT(1X, I10)
```

This blank does not appear on the line, however.

(b) Assuming implicit type variables, the statements

```
    WRITE (6,525) I, A
525 FORMAT(4X, I5, 10X, F10.2)
```

will cause the following to be printed:

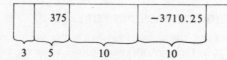

The first of the four blanks is used for carriage control.

Notes

1. Providing a larger field width for the first value to be printed in the given line than actually required by the number has the same effect as the initial X field. It is, however, less reliable.
2. It is not necessary to specify that blanks at the end of a line be provided; these columns are left blank automatically.

H. HOW TO SKIP LINES OR CARDS

A single FORTRAN statement may be used to handle more than one physical record (i.e., a line of print or a card with input data). This is accomplished explicitly with the use of slashes (/).

A closing parenthesis in a FORMAT statement terminates the current record. This means, among other things, that after a FORMAT statement is fully used to transfer the data specified by the corresponding input or output list (and the closing parenthesis is reached), the next sequential record is started.

Within a FORMAT statement, a slash may be used to cause the transition to the next record. In order to skip a line (or a card during an output operation), two slashes are used. The first terminates the current record, and the second causes the next record to be skipped.

The rules of record handling with the use of slashes in FORMAT statements are the following:

(1) If slashes are used at the beginning or at the end of a FORMAT statement, n slashes are required to skip n records (e.g., lines). This is so because the opening parenthesis causes the next record to be started, and the closing one terminates the current record.

(2) If slashes are used in the middle of a FORMAT statement, (n + 1) slashes are required to skip n records (since one slash is used to terminate the current record).

(3) No commas are needed to surround a slash.

EXAMPLE 5–8

Note the following statements:
(a)

```
    WRITE (6,543) I, J
543 FORMAT(1X, I10/1X, I10)
```

The two integers will be printed in two consecutive lines one under another.
(b)

```
    READ (5,517) R
517 FORMAT(//F10.2/)
```

Two cards will be skipped, a real number will be read, and subsequently, after the present card is terminated, the next card will be skipped.

I. HOW TO PRINT FIXED TEXT

To make the information presented during the output self-explanatory, it is often desirable to include its verbal description. Such description, in the form of a text prepared by the programmer, may be included in the FORMAT statement.

▷ FORTRAN 77 and many earlier implementations permit the following simple usage: In order to have the text printed, it is simply enclosed in apostrophes (single quotes) and placed in the FORMAT statement. If an apostrophe itself is to appear in the output, it is included in the FORMAT as a double apostrophe.

EXAMPLE 5-9

(a) In order to place centrally on a 132-column line of the line printer the value of WEIGHT, with the explanation of what it signifies, the following statement may be used:

```
     WRITE (6,589) WEIGHT
 589 FORMAT(50X, 'WEIGHT OF CARGO IS ', F9.2, ' LBS')
```

(b) To simply print a text (e.g., a heading), we may use

```
     WRITE (6, 571)
 571 FORMAT(54X, 'RESULTS OF EXPERIMENT XZ50')
```
◁

When apostrophe editing is not available, the alternative H edit descriptor may be used. Its general form is

$$\text{nH}\underbrace{\text{hh}\ldots\text{h}}_{n}$$

where n is the number of characters (represented by h) to be printed.

EXAMPLE 5-10

We may use

```
     WRITE (6,525) MEASUR, TOTAL
 525 FORMAT(5X, 8HTOTAL OF, I2, 8H EQUALS , F10.2)
```

to print the following line

```
      TOTAL OF 3 EQUALS     123.41
 ‿‿‿
  4
```

Note

1. how the blanks are included in the printed text;
2. that the variable name TOTAL is independent of the word TOTAL in the text.

Since care has to be exercised in counting characters for their inclusion in an edit descriptor, apostrophe editing should be used whenever available.

J. HOW TO SKIP TO THE TOP OF THE NEXT PAGE AND, IN GENERAL, CONTROL THE PRINTER CARRIAGE

When a line printer is used as the output device, the first character of every line sent for printing has to be a blank or another carriage control character, which is not printed.

It is usually desired that a new line be printed as the next line. This is specified by the blank as the carriage control character and may be accomplished in one of the following ways:

(1) Include 1X (or a wider blank field) as the first field descriptor in the FORMAT statement.

▷ (2) Use 1H☐ (or '☐' when apostrophe editing is available) as the first field descriptor in the FORMAT. ◁

(3) Provide too large a field width for the first number to be printed on a line (e.g., print 55 using I3).

Method (3) is error-prone (the number may happen to be too large) and should be avoided.

In general, to provide carriage control include the following field in a FORMAT statement as the first for a line:

▷ ' ' or 1H : write the immediate next line;
'0' or 1H0: advance two lines, i.e., skip one line;
'1' or 1H1: skip to the top of the next page;
'+' or 1H+: prevent line advancement, i.e., overprint the current line (used in graphical applications).

Apostrophe editing, available in FORTRAN 77 and similar implementations, is preferable. ◁

▷
EXAMPLE 5–11
When these statements are executed:

```
      WRITE (6,514)
  514 FORMAT(1H1, 45X, 5HTITLE)
or 514 FORMAT('1', 45X, 'TITLE')
```

the new page is started; 45 blanks are skipped, and the word TITLE is printed. ◁

K. MATCHING A FORMAT STATEMENT WITH AN INPUT OR OUTPUT LIST

A FORMAT statement may specify that several variables on the input or output list are to be edited in a repeating pattern. This is done by enclosing several edit descriptors in parentheses and providing a repeat specification before the group.

EXAMPLE 5-12

(a) The statement

501 FORMAT(2(I10, F10.2))

is equivalent to the statement

501 FORMAT(I10, F10.2, I10, F10.2)

(b) The statement

555 FORMAT(1X, 3(3X, I5), E8.1)

is equivalent to the statement

555 FORMAT(4X, I5, 3X, I5, 3X, I5, E8.1)

The numeric edit descriptors I, F, E, G contained in a FORMAT statement are used to transfer variables specified on the input or output lists of the corresponding READ or WRITE statements, respectively. These are applied from left to right, with the consideration of repeat specifications in front of the inner parentheses (if present).

If the number of variables in the input or output list is smaller than the number of the numeric edit descriptors in the corresponding FORMAT statement, the remaining descriptors are ignored. (This holds also for other edit descriptors, which will be introduced in later chapters.)

If the number of variables in the input or output list is greater than the number of descriptors, the FORMAT statement is reused. This means that when the closing parenthesis of the FORMAT statement is reached and there are variables remaining in the list:

(1) the current record (e.g., a card during an input) is terminated and the next record is started;

(2) the FORMAT statement is rescanned (reused, wholly or partially), until the input or output list is satisfied (or until a FORMAT error occurs). The reuse occurs as follows:

(a) If there are no other parentheses inside the enclosing parentheses of the FORMAT statement, the entire statement is reused.

(b) Otherwise, the FORMAT statement is reused from the left parenthesis that matches the rightmost right parenthesis within the overall enclosing parentheses of the statement (or from the repeat count, if it precedes it). For example, in the statement

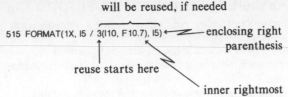

will be reused, if needed

515 FORMAT(1X, I5 / 3(I10, F10.7), I5) ← enclosing right parenthesis

reuse starts here

inner rightmost parenthesis

EXAMPLE 5-13

Implicit types of variables are assumed.

(a) Fewer variables than descriptors:

```
    WRITE (6,514) J, K, R, P
514 FORMAT(1X, 2I10 / 6E10.2)
```

The FORMAT will be executed as if it were

```
514 FORMAT(1X, 2I10/2E10.2)
```

(b) More variables than descriptors (input):

```
    READ (5,541) K, A, L, B
541 FORMAT(I10, E14.2)
```

The entire FORMAT statement will be used twice; for it to work correctly, however, the values of variables L and B have to be punched on a separate (second) card.

(c) More variables than descriptors (output):

```
    WRITE (6,517) K, I, R, M, Z
517 FORMAT(1X, I10, (1X, I10, F8.2))
```

The values of variables K, L, R will be printed on one line and the values of M and Z on the next. Note that the function of parentheses here is to set the reuse point.

Whenever possible, try to have the number of descriptors (repeated, if needed) match the number of variables on the input/output lists. This simplifies programming and thus averts errors.

Also, unless other considerations preclude it, try to use the same field descriptors for all program data of the given type. This practice will decrease the probability of error in the presentation of the data. For example,

```
512 FORMAT(3I10)
```

is preferable to

```
512 FORMAT(I7, I10, I8)
```

unless you have to economize on space.

L. USE OF INPUT/OUTPUT STATEMENTS TO CHECK FOR ERRORS AND END OF INPUT DATA (FORTRAN 77)

FORTRAN 77 (as well as some earlier implementations) allows the programmer to check for special conditions such as an input/output error and end of data.

To check for an input/output error, the following is used:

READ (unit number, FORMAT label, ERR = label)
WRITE (unit number, FORMAT label, ERR = label)

where ERR = label specifies the label of the program statement to which the control is to revert if an error occurs. An input/output error takes place when the data cannot be read/written with the given edit descriptor; for example, if a real number is encountered when an I edit descriptor is to be applied. If no ERR disposition is included in the READ or WRITE statement, the program will be terminated. For example, the statement

READ (5,512, ERR = 120)

specifies that if an input error occurs, the control is to pass to the program statement labeled 120. This and the following statements may print an error message and, possibly, attempt to correct the error.

To check for the end of input data, the following is used:

READ (device number, FORMAT label, END = label)

where END = label specifies the label of the statement to which the control is to pass if no more data are available to be read. This option is used, for example, when multiple cards are to be read, instead of including a special trailer (sentinel) data card as the last data card. In the latter case the program would have to test the data in every card. If the END specifier is included, the system automatically transfers control to the given program statement when the control card that signifies the end of the job (i.e., end of data, see Chapter 6–B–1) is encountered. Starting with this statement, all the data are available to the program.

Both ERR and END specifiers may be used in a READ statement, for example,

READ (5,577, ERR = 220, END = 50)

6

PROCESSING OF NUMERICAL DATA. ADVANCED FEATURES

The discussion of the manipulation of numerical data is continued from Chapter 4. It should be appreciated, however, that the facilities introduced in the present chapter are used to process also nonnumerical data, as will be seen in Chapter 9.

The application and use of arrays—aggregates of data items of the same type and bearing the same name—are explained.

The use of the DATA statement for the initialization of variables and array elements is discussed.

Frequently needed arithmetic (and other) routines are included in every FORTRAN system in the form of intrinsic (built-in) functions. Their use considerably simplifies the programmer's task.

Two or more names may be assigned to the same memory location(s) with the use of the EQUIVALENCE statement. This, in certain cases, results in a saving of memory space and may make a program more readable.

Two special types of arithmetic data, double precision and complex, are sometimes applied.

A. ARRAYS

Arrays are ordered collections of data items of the same type and with the same name. Individual array elements are identified by their subscripts, which appear in parentheses after the array name. The number of subscripts corresponds to the number of dimensions in the given array. In FORTRAN, arrays have to be declared in a type or a DIMENSION statement before they may be used. An array declaration specifies the number of its dimensions and the size of each of them. The arrays are manipulated through their elements; uniform manipulation of array elements calls for the use of loops. The manipulation of individual array elements is similar to the manipulation of variables.

FORTRAN arrays are stored in memory in the column order. A general tool for their input and output is the implied-DO list.

1. WHAT AN ARRAY IS

In order to manipulate a collection of data items in a uniform fashion, we may name them with a single name. Each item is then identified by its position in the collection.

Such a collection of data items of the same type bearing a single name is called an *array;* individual data items are *array elements.* An array element has a value of a given type, like any variable; its other characteristic is, however, its position within the array. This position is identified by the *subscripts* of the array element. In many respects an array element is an equivalent of a variable and is thus often also called a *subscripted variable.*

An array element has as many subscripts as the array has *dimensions;* a subscript identifies the position of the element of the array along each dimension.

▷ The old FORTRAN standard allowed for arrays with up to three dimensions. FORTRAN 77 allows up to seven dimensions in an array. ◁

The use of arrays is understood best by considering their applications.

A. ONE-DIMENSIONAL ARRAYS

When a sequential ordering of a collection of data is required, a one-dimensional array (also called a *vector* or linear array) is used. It corresponds to a vector in algebra.

EXAMPLE 6–1

We have a list of temperature measurements taken in a room every hour. In order to manipulate these data (e.g., to chart them or to find statistical measures) it is convenient to represent them as a real vector TEMP(I), where the subscript I indicates the number of the measurement (see Fig. 6–1).

I = 1	67.11
I = 2	66.71
.	.
.	.

For example,
the value of TEMP (2) is 66.71

| I = 150 | 68.18 |

FIGURE 6–1. A one-dimensional array (vector): TEMP(I)

Note the dependence between the subscript of an array element (e.g., 2), which serves to identify the element, and the value of the element (e.g., 66.71).

B. TWO-DIMENSIONAL ARRAYS

When an element of an array has to be classified according to two characteristics, a two-dimensional array is used. Each of the two subscripts specifies the position of the element according to the corresponding characteristic.

EXAMPLE 6-2

The experiment described in Example 6–1 is modified so that the room temperature measurement taken every hour is triplicated (three copies, replicas, of every measurement are obtained).

For the reason of further processing, it is desired to identify every measurement by two characteristics: its number among the hourly measurements and its position within the triple readings taken at this particular hour.

The array shown in Fig. 6–2 results:

Number of hourly measurement (I)	Number of replica (J) 1	2	3	
1	65.18	65.01	65.21	← TEMP(1, 3)
2	66.13	65.98	66.04	
.	.	.	.	
.	.	.	.	
.	.	.	.	
150	67.01	66.85	66.89	

FIGURE 6-2. A two-dimensional array (matrix): TEMP(I, J)

Note that the first subscript (I) identifies the row of the array element, and the second (J) identifies its column. For example, the second replica of the first measurement may be retrieved as TEMP(1, 2); its value is 65.01.

A two-dimensional array corresponds to an algebraic matrix and thus is often called a *matrix;* in mathematical notation the subscripts of an element are usually written below the line (e.g., $TEMP_{12}$).

C. THREE- AND HIGHER-DIMENSIONAL ARRAYS

When every data item collected in the array has three classifying characteristics, three subscripts are needed to identify the element. A collection of such elements is a three-dimensional array.

EXAMPLE 6–3

The experiment of Examples 6–1 and 6–2 is further modified to measure the room temperature every hour, in triplicate, by measuring both at the floor and at the ceiling.

The results are then stored in a three-dimensional array that may be represented graphically as a cube (see Fig. 6–3).

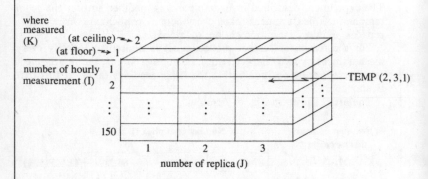

FIGURE 6–3. A three-dimensional array: TEMP (I, J, K)

Note that the total number of elements (i.e., measurements in our case) equals $I \times J \times K$.

▷ If more than three characteristics classify the elements of the array, higher-dimensional arrays may be used (if available in the given FORTRAN implementation). Such need arises rather infrequently. ◁

2. DECLARATION OF ARRAYS

An array occupies a number of locations in the memory of a computer. Since in a FORTRAN system the allocation of memory space is performed during the compilation (translation) of the program, a declaration (i.e., a nonexecutable statement informing the compiler) is necessary to specify the type of the array and the maximum number of elements in it. This declaration may be either a DIMENSION statement or an ordinary type statement.

The general form of the declaration is thus either of these:

DIMENSION array name(dimension specification), . . .
INTEGER array name (dimension specification), . . .
REAL array name (dimension specification), . . .

Arrays may be constituted of data of any type defined in FORTRAN, as will be seen later. Their declarations follow these rules.

(1) An array name is formed like any other symbolic name in FOR-TRAN (see the list before Example 3–1) and has to be unique among the symbolic names in the program unit.

(2) A DIMENSION statement may be used to declare any number of arrays of various types. It does not define the type of the array, which thus has to be defined implicitly (through the starting letter) or explicitly. If a DIMENSION statement is used, in order to define explicitly the type of the array, its name (*alone*) is to be placed in an appropriate type statement.

(3) If an array is fully specified through a type statement, no DIMEN-SION statement is required. Thus, the dimensions of the array have to be specified as integer constants either in a type or in a DIMEN-SION statement, but not in both.

(4) A type statement (e.g., REAL) may contain any number of array and variable names.

(5) DIMENSION statements, which are nonexecutable, have to precede all executable statements in the program unit (e.g., they may be placed immediately after the type statements).

For example, to declare a two-dimensional real array of 1000 elements LIQUID(10, 100), we may use one of the two methods:

```
REAL LIQUID
DIMENSION LIQUID(10, 100)
```

or

```
REAL LIQUID(10, 100)
```

Thus, both the type of the array and the number of its elements are specified.

It is more convenient to use type statements than DIMENSION statements to declare arrays, since always only one statement is required.

Array dimensions are specified as follows:

(1) Dimensions have to be specified by integer constants.

▷ (2) Up to three dimensions are allowed by the old standard, and up to seven by FORTRAN 77. ◁

(3) Constants that specify particular dimensions have to be separated by commas.

(4) Dimensions are specified as their upper bounds (i.e., the highest values of the subscript). The lower bound is assumed to be 1.

For example, in the array LIQUID(10, 100) the first dimension ranges from 1 to 10 and the second from 1 to 100.

In the case of such specification, all the subscripts of array elements are positive and start at 1. The size of each dimension equals the value specified (i.e., the size of the dimension of LIQUID is 10). This is the only way to declare arrays in FORTRAN IV.

▷ FORTRAN 77 permits an alternative way to specify the dimensions of an array, stating their lower and upper bounds separated by a semicolon. Moreover, the subscripts of the array elements may have negative or zero values. For example, this is a legal array declaration in FORTRAN 77:

```
INTEGER WEIGHT(-5:25, 0:100), HEIGHT(10, 5:90)
```

Such specification is sometimes desirable due to the meaning of the subscripts in the problem context.

Note that the two methods of specification may be combined (for example, the first dimension of the array HEIGHT implicitly ranges from 1 to 10). When the two bounds are specified, the size of a dimension is equal:

upper bound − lower bound + 1 ◁

EXAMPLE 6-4

The following are valid declarations of the integer array INCOME:

```
DIMENSION INCOME(10, 25)
```

or

```
INTEGER INCOME(10, 25)
```

(but not both!)

To declare a real array of the same name, we would have to use:

```
REAL INCOME
DIMENSION INCOME(10, 25)
```

or, more simply,

```
REAL INCOME(10, 25)
```

▷ The following declaration would be valid only in FORTRAN 77:

REAL INCOME(6:15, −24:0)   ◁

Be careful in declaring the size of an array. Obviously, it has to suffice for the application. Limit it to the space really necessary, however. A statement like

DIMENSION X(100, 1000)

will almost certainly exceed the memory space available for your program.

---

3. SUBSCRIPTS AND ARRAY ELEMENTS

Arrays are manipulated through their elements. A single element is manipulated in the same way as a variable.

To manipulate part or all of the array elements in the same fashion, loops are used (see Chapter 7) in order to implement the following construct

> **while** there are more elements in the array **do**
>   **begin**
>   get the next array element;
>   manipulate it
>   **end**

An array element (subscripted variable) may be used essentially anywhere in place of an ordinary variable of the same type, i.e., in expressions and input or output lists, as mentioned in Chapters 4 and 5.

A particular array element is identified by its subscripts. As many subscript values as there are dimensions in the given array have to be specified. The values of the subscripts have to fall within the limits declared by the dimension specification for the array.

"Subscript out of bounds" is one of the most frequent errors in the manipulation of arrays.

EXAMPLE 6–5

Following the type statement

REAL LIQUID(10, 100), DOUBLE

an element of the array LIQUID may be used as follows:

DOUBLE = 2. * LIQUID(5, 15)

Note that in the array declaration the parenthesized numbers signify dimensions of the array, while in an executable statement they are subscripts of the particular array element. For example, the statement

    TRIPLE = 3. * LIQUID(10, 100)

refers to the last element of the array.

A subscript may be an integer constant or variable or, in general, an integer expression.

▷ FORTRAN 77 permits any integer-valued expression to be used as subscript, while FORTRAN IV limits it to the following forms:

    variable ± constant
    constant * variable
    constant–1 * variable ± constant–2   ◁

If a subscript is other than a constant, first the value of this subscript is obtained during the program execution. Only then is the value of the array element manipulated.

EXAMPLE 6–6

If J is an integer variable whose current value is 2, TEMP(2) and TEMP(3*J−4) refer to the same element of the array TEMP.

4. HOW FORTRAN ARRAYS ARE STORED IN MEMORY

The elements of arrays declared in FORTRAN programs are stored in consecutive memory locations so that their leftmost subscripts vary most rapidly. For a vector, this is the natural way of element storage.

EXAMPLE 6–7

The elements of the vector declared

    REAL GRADES(10)

are stored in this order:

    GRADES(1), GRADES(2), ..., GRADES(10)

For a two-dimensional array (matrix), this is the *column order* of storage: the array is stored column by column.

EXAMPLE 6–8

The elements of the matrix declared as follows:

    INTEGER PRESS(2, 3)

are stored in this order:

    PRESS(1, 1), PRESS(2, 1), PRESS(1, 2), PRESS(2, 2), PRESS(1, 3), PRESS(2, 3)

This storage order determines the order of the input/output of arrays as described below.

5. INPUT/OUTPUT OF ARRAYS

To input or output a single array element, it is placed on the appropriate input or output list, as a variable would be.

EXAMPLE 6-9

If J is an integer variable with a defined value and LIQUID is a real array, these are valid statements:

```
     READ (5,511) V, LIQUID(5, J)
 511 FORMAT(F10.0, 5X, F12.4)
```

To input or output the *entire* array, its name *without any subscripts* may be placed in the appropriate input or output list. (This is one of the few cases when an array name may appear in a program by itself). The array elements have to be presented for input in the FORTRAN storage order (see Section A–4 above); they also appear in this order during output.

The input/output process is controlled by the FORMAT statement in the case of formatted input/output.

EXAMPLE 6-10

For the input of the entire array SALES that has been declared as

```
     INTEGER SALES(50, 50)
```

the statements

```
     READ (5,553) SALES
 553 FORMAT(8F10.2)
```

may be used.

This FORMAT statement corresponds to the placement of eight array elements per card. The FORMAT statement will be used repeatedly until the entire 2500-element array SALES has been read in. This means that 313 cards will be read, the last of which contains only four data items. Had we used

```
 553 FORMAT(F10.2)
```

only one data item would have to be placed on each card, and 2500 would have been required.

The general method of array input/output is the *implied-DO list,*† a construct that is placed in an input or output list and has one of two general forms:

(array-name(index), index = initial value, final value)

† Since the implied-DO list is a special case of the FORTRAN loop (DO) construct, some readers may find it helpful to consult Chapter 7–E on some of the more detailed points.

or, rarely,

(array-name(index), index = initial value, final value, increment)

For example,

READ (5,543) (TEMP(I), I = 1, 100)

or

WRITE (6,517) (TEMP(K), K = 1, 100, 2)

Such lists imply that the values of the array elements are to be read or written beginning with the subscript of the initial value and ending with the subscript of the final value. If no increment is included, it is assumed to be 1, otherwise the next values of the subscript are obtained by adding this increment to the previous value. When the resulting subscript becomes greater than the final value, the input or output stops. This method may be used to input or output the whole or a part of an array in a desired order.

> **EXAMPLE 6-11**
>
> (a)
>
> READ (5,505) (ARR(I), I = 1, 50)
>
> will input the array elements in the following order:
>
> ARR(1), ARR(2), . . . , ARR(50)
>
> (b)
>
> WRITE (6,505) (ARR(3, J), J = 4, 20, 5)
>
> will output the elements of the two-dimensional array in the following order:
>
> ARR(3, 4), ARR(3, 9), ARR(3, 14), ARR(3, 19)

▷ In FORTRAN IV, all index values should be integer constants or variables greater than 0. FORTRAN 77 allows also the use of expressions (see Chapter 7).

Since the implied-DO list represents a special use of the DO loop construct, minor differences exist in its definition between the old standard and FORTRAN 77. The latter allows for a more general form of index values and guards from empty loops. For a precise description of the DO loops in FORTRAN 77, see Chapter 7-E. ◁

A single index may be used to control input or output of more than one array, as shown in the following example.

EXAMPLE 6–12

The statement

WRITE (6,505) (M, K, X(M), Y(M, 3), M = 2, 4)

will cause the output of data items in the following order:

2, K, X(2), Y(2, 3), 3, K, X(3), Y(3, 3), 4, K, X(4), Y(4, 3)

Note that the value not controlled by the index is simply repeated (which may be desired during an output, but almost never during an input). The implied-DO list may be placed anywhere in the input or output list in keeping with the desired order of input or output, which proceeds from the left to the right of the list.

EXAMPLE 6–13

This important example stresses that the value is assigned to a variable immediately after input:

READ (5,505) M, (X(I), I = 1, M)

is a valid statement. The length of the array X is known when its input starts, since the value of M has been read in beforehand.

The statement below is, however, invalid:

READ (5,505) (M, X(I), I = 1, M)

since the implied-DO list constitutes a single entity.

Implied-DO lists may be nested (placed within one another) to transfer the contents of multidimensional arrays A set of parentheses and a comma are needed for every index.

The innermost index changes fastest. This is illustrated by the following example.

EXAMPLE 6–14

The following statement reads in a two-dimensional array in column order (which should be used to present input data, since it is the order in which arrays are stored in FORTRAN):

READ (5,505) ((X(I, J), I = 1, 5), J = 1, 10)

which results in the following order:

X(1, 1), X(2, 1), . . . ,X(5, 1),X(1, 2),X(2, 2), . . . ,X(5, 2), . . . ,X(5, 10)

On the other hand, this statement causes the row order output of the same array:

WRITE (6,505) ((X(I, J), J = 1, 10), I = 1, 5)

in the following order:

X(1, 1), X(1, 2), . . . ,X(1, 10),X(2, 1), . . . ,X(2, 10), . . . ,X(5, 10)

The following statement reads in a three-dimensional array in column order:

```
READ (5,505) (((Y(I, J, K), I = 1, 5), J = 1, 10), K = 1, 25)
```

Note the matching of parentheses and the use of commas in nested DO lists.

If formatted input/output is used, the layout of data on the external medium (e.g., cards or print lines) is described by the corresponding FORMAT statement. The closing parenthesis of this FORMAT statement terminates the current record (as explained in Chapter 5–K). The new records are started until the input or output list is exhausted (or an error occurs).

EXAMPLE 6–15

(a) The statement

```
READ (5,505) (LENGTH(I), I = 1, 100)
```

with

```
505 FORMAT(I10)
```

will read 100 cards with the value of one array element on a card. On the other hand, with

```
505 FORMAT(5I10)
```

20 cards will be read, with five values per card.
(b) The statements

```
WRITE (6,507) ((ARR(I, J), J = 1, 8), I = 1, 10)
507 FORMAT(1X, 8F9.2)
```

will cause 10 lines to be printed, with one eight-element row of the array ARR per line.

B. INITIALIZATION OF VARIABLES AND ARRAY ELEMENTS

Before the value of a variable or of an array element is used, it has to be defined. This means that no variable may appear, for example, in an expression or in an output list before it acquires a value.

The failure to assign a value to a variable (or array element) before its use is one of the most common programming mistakes.

A variable or an array element may be assigned a value during the program execution. Most frequently it is done in one of the following ways:

by an assignment statement in which this variable or an array element appears on the left-hand side;

by a READ statement in which it appears on the input list.

It is sometimes desirable to preassign certain values when the program is being written, instead of reading them in during the execution. A DATA statement provides such an alternative way of assigning values to variables and array elements. Thus, a DATA statement serves to initialize variables and arrays: their values are assigned before the program execution starts. This statement has the following general form:

DATA list of variable, array element, or array names/list of values to be assigned/

▷ These two lists may be repeated after a comma (the comma is optional in FORTRAN 77).

Standard FORTRAN IV does not allow the placing of array names in a DATA statement; thus the individual array elements have to be listed in order to be initialized. ◁

For example,

```
DATA I/5/, A(3), A(7)/25.1, 14.2/
```

initializes the variable I to 5 and the array elements A(3) to 25.1 and A(7) to 14.2.

In the assignment of values, the following hold:

(1) The type of values to be assigned has to correspond to the type of variables or arrays.

(2) The same value may be assigned to a number of entities by prefacing it with the integer that specifies the number of repetitions and an asterisk (i.e., n*).

(3) An array name stands for all of its elements in the column order.

(4) The number of entities in the first list must equal the number of values in the second one.

EXAMPLE 6–16

The following illustrates the use of the DATA statement:

```
INTEGER I, ARR(10, 15)
REAL X, Y, VAL(2)
DATA I, ARR, X, Y/125, 150*0, 0.31E−3, 1.2/, VAL(1),
+       VAL(2)/0.,0.5/
```

Establish the correspondence between the entities and the values.

▷ In FORTRAN 77, implied-DO lists (see Chapter 6–A–5) may be used in the lists of variables and array elements; for example,

```
DATA (VAL(I), I = 11, 100)/90*0./
```

Since old FORTRAN IV does not allow implied-DO lists or array names to appear in the first list, explicit listing of all array elements to be initialized must occur. ◁

Nonexecutable DATA statements have to be placed after specification statements such as type statements.

---

(1) It is a good practice to place the DATA statement *immediately* after specification statements (e.g., following DIMENSION statements).
(2) The DATA statement *only* initializes the value of a variable or an array element *before* the execution. If this value is subsequently changed *during* the execution, the effect of the DATA statement ceases, since it cannot be executed. The use of DATA statements to initialize variables often leads to mistakes flowing from the programmer's failure to recognize this fact.
The DATA statement is particularly useful when employed to assign names to the values that will remain constant throughout the program execution. In particular, it may serve to avoid "magic numbers" in the program, i.e., constants whose significance is unknown to the reader. Thus, for example, the statement

    DATA PI/3.14/

will help in understanding the program in which the constant value is used.

C. INTRINSIC FUNCTIONS

Certain programming tasks, such as, for example, computing a square root or an exponential of a real number, frequently repeat themselves. In order to simplify programmers' work, sequences of statements that perform these tasks have been written by the designers of the FORTRAN system and have been included as built-in modules.

Thus, FORTRAN provides a number of predefined (built-in) program modules that compute a single value when presented with one or more other values, called arguments. These modules, each performing a particular task, are called *intrinsic functions*. Most of these functions compute certain mathematical functions or perform type conversions.

Modular programming in FORTRAN is described as a general facility in Chapter 8. Since the intrinsic functions do not have to be defined by the programmer, their use is very simple. They may be used essentially anywhere in the program instead of variables of the same type. A function reference has the following general form:

function name (argument(s))

where the number of arguments and their types are fixed for any given function (see Table 6–1).

For example,

X = SQRT(Y)

In general, an argument may be an expression of the given type and as such may itself contain function references. For example, in the assignment statement

DISCR = SQRT(B ** 2 − 4. * A * FLOAT(K))

the real function SQRT is used; its argument contains a reference to another function, FLOAT. The value that results from the evaluation of a function is assigned to its name (here, SQRT).

▷ FORTRAN 77 specifies both the so-called generic and the specific name for a function. When the same computation is required for different types of values, different specific functions are used (see the special functions in Table 6–1). In FORTRAN 77, a single generic name may be used instead, with the translator substituting automatically the required specific name.

FORTRAN IV and other implementations of the old standard use only specific names. ◁

It is advisable to use the specific names for the reason of program portability.

The most useful functions of integer and real arguments are presented in Table 6–1. FORTRAN systems also contain a number of functions operating on other numeric data types. The functions of character arguments are discussed in Chapter 9.

Note the following:

(1) Most functions require a single argument. If more than one argument is required, all arguments are of the same type.

(2) All the functions presented in Table 6–1, with the exception of conversions, render the result (i.e., acquire the value) of the same type as the argument(s).

Use the functions IFIX and FLOAT for explicit conversions, to avoid mixed-mode expressions and assignment statements with two sides of different types.

When a function reference is used in an expression, the value of the function is obtained as the matter of first-order precedence.

TABLE 6-1. Important intrinsic functions of integer and real arguments

GENERIC NAME (FORTRAN 77 ONLY)	SPECIFIC NAME (FORTRAN 77 AND FORTRAN IV)	TYPE AND NUMBER OF ARGUMENTS	TYPE OF FUNCTION (RESULT)	FUNCTION PERFORMED
		algebraic functions		
SQRT	SQRT	real, 1	real	square root: $\sqrt{x}$
EXP	EXP	real, 1	real	exponential: e^x
LOG	ALOG	real, 1	real	natural log: $\log x$
LOG10	ALOG10	real, 1	real	common log: $\log_{10}x$
		important trigonometric functions (the arguments should be expressed in radians; 1 radian $\simeq 57°$		
SIN	SIN	real, 1	real	sine
COS	COS	real, 1	real	cosine
TAN	TAN	real, 1	real	tangent
		special functions		
ABS	IABS	integer, 1	integer	absolute value: $|x|$
	ABS	real, 1	real	absolute value: $|x|$
MAX	MAX0	integer, $\geqslant 2$	integer	largest value
	AMAX1	real, $\geqslant 2$	real	largest value
MIN	MIN0	integer, $\geqslant 2$	integer	smallest value
	AMIN1	real, $\geqslant 2$		smallest value
MOD	MOD	integer, 2	integer $\}$	arg-1—integer part of
	AMOD	real, 2	real $\}$	(arg-1/arg-2) *arg-2
		conversions between integer and real values		
INT	IFIX	real, 1	integer	truncate fraction
REAL	FLOAT	integer, 1	real	convert to real (no value change)

EXAMPLE 6-17

Some of the functions of Table 6-1 are used here.
Assume implicit variable types.

V = EXP(SQRT(X))   represents $v = e^{\sqrt{x}}$

Z = AMAX1(2. * A, 5.)   represents $z = \max(2a,5)$

V = SQRT(FLOAT(IABS(K - 3)))   represents $v = \sqrt{|k-3|}$

D. MEMORY SHARING THROUGH THE USE
OF EQUIVALENCE†

It is sometimes desired to have more than one symbolic name referring to the same memory location. For example, we may want to have two variable names referring to the same entity or an alternative name referring to a part of an array. This, arranged with the use of the EQUIVALENCE statement, occurs essentially in two distinct situations.

(1) Provision of alternative names for the same data;
- (a) A part of an array has a special meaning within a program and is to be manipulated separately from the rest of the array. For example, in an array that holds the series of temperature readings taken at 10-minute intervals within 24 hours, the nightly data are to be processed separately [see Example 6–18(c) below].
- (b) Due to an oversight, two distinct names are used in a program for the same entity (a variable or an array). Temporarily, until the oversight is corrected, an EQUIVALENCE statement may be used to make the two names refer to the same location(s).

(2) Saving memory space; the following situation may call for the use of an EQUIVALENCE statement: Two arrays of the same (or approximately the same) size are required by a given program. One of them is utilized at the beginning of the program and is then no longer needed; the second is used afterwards. The same space (or the larger of the two required) may be assigned to the two arrays, since they never use the space simultaneously.

Since FORTRAN compilers allocate the space for arrays statically (with a minor exception), i.e., before the program execution begins, this usage results in a memory saving.

The EQUIVALENCE statement should be used with great care as it often leads to subtle, and hence difficult to find, mistakes. Unless you have an important reason to do so (e.g., lack of memory space), do not use it.

The EQUIVALENCE statement has the following general form:

EQUIVALENCE (equivalence list), . . . , (equivalence list)

where an equivalence list may include names of variables, array elements,

† This and the remaining two sections of this chapter may be skipped without loss of continuity.

or arrays separated by commas. The entries in every such list are thus made to refer to the same item. For example,

```
EQUIVALENCE (K, L), (ARR(10), BLOCK(20))
```

▷ The old standard requires that all array subscripts be integer constants; FORTRAN 77 allows as subscripts also expressions that include only integer constants. ◁

The nonexecutable EQUIVALENCE statement is placed before all executable statements in the program unit (for example, after the type and DIMENSION statements). In a subprogram (see below in Chapter 8), dummy arguments may not appear in an EQUIVALENCE statement.

Every equivalence list ought to include at least two names that are thus made equivalent. In this fashion, every list (if there is more than one) establishes a separate equivalence among the entities named in it.

While the programmer is not precluded from placing in the same equivalence lists items of different types, such use should be reserved for exceptional situations.

The EQUIVALENCE statement ensures that the entities specified in a list refer to the same locations. Since arrays are always placed in consecutive locations in the column-first order (see Chapter 6–A–4), when arrays or their elements are specified in an equivalence list, the remaining array elements are also made equivalent in the order of their placement in memory.

When an array name alone is placed in an equivalence list, its first element is associated with others [see Example 6–18(b) below].

EXAMPLE 6–18

(a) The statements

```
REAL X, Y(50)
EQUIVALENCE (X, Y(23))
```

give the element with the subscript 23 of the array Y the alternative name X.

(b) The statements

```
INTEGER ITEM(30), GRADES(20)
EQUIVALENCE(ITEM, GRADES(11))
```

establish the following correspondence:

```
        ITEM(1)        ITEM (2)  ...  ITEM(20)  ...  ITEM(30)
          ↕               ↕             ↕
GRADES(1) ... GRADES(11)   GRADES(12) ... GRADES(20)
```

Thus, these arrays overlap in memory.

(c) We have temperature readings taken at 10-minute intervals over a 24-hour period starting at 1 p.m. It is desired to identify the measurement taken during the night (11 p.m.–7 a.m.). This is accomplished as follows:

```
REAL TEMP(145), NIGHT(49)
EQUIVALENCE (TEMP(60), NIGHT(1))
```

Thus, we do not need to duplicate the contents of the array TEMP, but instead assign an alternative name NIGHT to its part.

Since an EQUIVALENCE statement assigns alternative names to actual elements, it cannot attempt to establish a physically impossible correspondence.

EXAMPLE 6–19

The following EQUIVALENCE statement makes contradictory demands:

```
REAL A(5), B(10)
EQUIVALENCE (A, B(3)), (A(2), B)
```

Analyze it.

E. DOUBLE PRECISION DATA

In some applications, the precision (i.e., the number of significant digits) available with the use of real data in a given system is not sufficient. In this case, double precision constants, variables, and arrays may be employed instead. While the exact number of significant digits in double precision data depends on the implementation, it is usually about double the precision of real data, and thus at least 14.

Do not use double precision needlessly since such values usually occupy twice the memory space of real data and take longer for the computer to manipulate.

A double precision constant is written in exponential form, with the letter D separating the exponent from the mantissa (instead of E as in a real number—see Chapter 4–A). For example,

```
123.4567100012D–8
```

where the letter D indicates that the number preceding it should be multiplied by 10 to the power of the number that follows D.

Double precision variables and arrays have to be explicitly declared with a DOUBLE PRECISION type statement:

DOUBLE PRECISION GAMMA, DELTA(10, 10)

To input or output double precision data, a D edit descriptor is used; it has the general form

Dw.d

and operates precisely as the E descriptor (see Chapter 5–E and 5–F), the only difference being that the exponent is separated by D instead of E on the input or output medium.

Double precision expressions are evaluated according to the usual rules (see Chapter 4–C).

▷ If an implementation allows for mixing double precision and real data types (as FORTRAN 77 does), the representation of the real number is automatically converted to double precision, without change in value. ◁

If an assignment of a double precision value to a real variable is performed, the value is truncated.

Several intrinsic functions deal with double precision values; some of these should be used for explicit conversions between them and real data.

F. COMPLEX DATA

A complex number z

$$z = a + bi$$

consists of two values, its real (a) and imaginary (b) parts. (The word "real" has here a special meaning.) If a pair of real numbers is declared to constitute a single complex number, it may be read in as such, manipulated automatically according to the rules of complex arithmetic, and the results may be presented as output.

A complex constant is an ordered pair of real-type constants, separated by a comma and enclosed in parentheses. For example, two complex constants are

(5.371,3.111)   (2.1E−9,55.3)

Complex variables and arrays have to be explicitly declared with a COMPLEX type statement, for example,

COMPLEX IMPEDN, ARR(50, 3)

A complex data item is treated for the purposes of input/output as two real-type numbers.

EXAMPLE 6–20

The following sequence of statements:

```
      COMPLEX IMPEDN
      READ (5,511) IMPEDN
  511 FORMAT(F10.2, 5X, F10.2)
```

assigns a value to the complex variable IMPEDN.

Any real-type edit descriptor (F, E, or G) may be used in accordance with the rules specified for real numbers (see Chapter 5–E and 5–F).

Real-type operands may be mixed with complex ones; the former are then automatically converted to complex form with a zero imaginary part. Explicit conversions with special intrinsic function are preferred.

7

CONTROL OF
PROGRAM EXECUTION FLOW

The statements that control execution flow are essential to any nontrivial program. They make it possible to provide alternative paths for program execution (a decision construct) and to provide for reuse of program statements to achieve a cumulative effect (a loop).

The following are the essential statements native to FORTRAN that control the execution flow:

> GOTO (unconditional transfer of control)
> STOP and CONTINUE
> logical IF

▷   block IF construct in FORTRAN 77   ◁

> DO
> computed GOTO
> arithmetic IF

The basic constructs of structured programming may be easily built as follows:

▷   **if-then-else:** available directly in FORTRAN 77 as the block IF construct; otherwise may be built with logical IF statements;   ◁

> **while-do** and **repeat-until** loops: built with logical IF statements;
> indexed loop: available directly as the DO loop;
> **case:** built with a computed GOTO statement.

A. UNCONDITIONAL TRANSFER OF CONTROL (GOTO)

When the next statement to be executed in a program is different than the next one in the text of the program, the

GOTO label

statement is inserted to divert the flow of control to the statement bearing the given label.

Thus the GOTO (sometimes written as GO TO) statement causes the control to branch around one or more program statements; for example,

GOTO 30   20 X = X + 1.

$$\cdot$$

30 X = X + 1.   GOTO 20

The goal of a GOTO statement can only be an executable statement. After the unconditional control transfer, the program execution continues from the statement to which the control has been transferred.

EXAMPLE 7-1

A practicable, but undesirable, way to stop the execution of a FORTRAN program is for it to run out of input data: when a READ statement is executed and no more data are found, the program is stopped. In the following problem this—not recommended—method is employed to illustrate the use of the GOTO statement.

Problem

For every record (i.e., card)—each one holds three real numbers—the average value is to be obtained.

Solution

The flowchart of the solution is shown in Fig. 7-1.

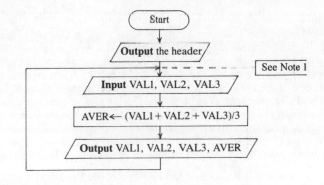

FIGURE 7-1.

The program follows.

```
C    PROGRAM: AVERAGE
C    AUTHOR:              DATE:
C
C    AVERAGES ARE COMPUTED FOR SETS OF 3 REAL NUMBERS
C    (PROGRAM STOPS BY RUNNING OUT OF DATA - NOT RECOMMENDED)
C
C    VAL1, VAL2, VAL3 - NUMBERS TO BE AVERAGED
C    AVER - AVERAGE OF 3 NUMBERS
C
        IMPLICIT REAL (A-Z)
C    PRINT HEADER ON NEW PAGE
        WRITE (6, 501)
  501 FORMAT('1', 25X, 'NUMBERS', 17X, 'AVERAGE')
C
C    OBTAIN NUMBERS AND PRINT THEM WITH THEIR AVERAGE
   10 READ (5, 502) VAL1, VAL2, VAL3
  502      FORMAT(3F10.2)
           AVER = (VAL1 + VAL2 + VAL3) / 3.
           WRITE (6, 503) VAL1, VAL2, VAL3, AVER
  503      FORMAT(10X, 3(F10.2, 2X), F10.2)
        GOTO 10
        STOP
        END
```

A sample printout:

	NUMBERS		AVERAGE
15.10	13.10	12.40	13.53
16.70	5.90	4.10	8.90
9.60	0.30	0.70	3.53

Notes

1. Looking at the flowchart of Fig. 7–1, we observe that there seems to be no provision for program termination. If it were indeed so, the program would be in an infinite loop. In our case, however, the program will be terminated by the FORTRAN system when it runs out of data: if there are N sets of three numbers each, the statement labeled 10 will be executed $N + 1$ times. During the last execution of this statement the program will be terminated. It is, however, improper to rely on such features of the system.

2. What are the methods of ensuring that the execution will terminate correctly when the number of records is not known beforehand?

   a. If it is available, as in FORTRAN 77, use the END = option in the READ statement (see Chapter 5–L).

   b. Otherwise, include as the last data card a trailer (sentinel) card that contains a special data item, which cannot be one of the processed items. Then, use an IF statement (see Section D below) to check for it before computing the average value.

3. Note that the statements between 10 and GOTO 10 have been indented: this makes it easier to see the structure of the program.

In a flowchart, GOTO is shown simply as a flowline.

Undisciplined use of GOTO's should be avoided, in particular, in transferring execution flow backward. Before using a GOTO, think whether the program logic cannot be more clearly expressed without it. Unconditional transfer of control often confuses the logic of the program and makes it difficult to understand, test, and modify.

As will be seen later in this chapter, the GOTO statement may be used to implement several control structures not available directly in FORTRAN. Such disciplined use of GOTO's helps to organize a FORTRAN program into a readable text. For a general discussion of control structures to be used in programming, see Chapter 2.

B. CONTINUE STATEMENT

An executable statement of the general form

label CONTINUE

may be used anywhere in the program where a labeled executable statement is needed. (While the statement does not have to be labeled, its essential function is that of a label carrier.)

This statement does not in itself change any values or influence the flow of control. It is used as a delimiting statement in several control structures presented in this chapter.

EXAMPLE 7-2

In this code fragment

```
        .
        .
        .
      GOTO 10
        .
        .
        .
   10 CONTINUE
        .
        .
        .
```

all the statements between GOTO and CONTINUE are skipped.

C. TERMINATION OF EXECUTION

The program is terminated when the statement

STOP

is executed.

There may be several such executable statements in the program text; in that case it is convenient to use an alternative form:

STOP   n

where n is an integer of five or fewer digits. When the first STOP statement is encountered by the program execution flow, the program is terminated and the number n is printed; thus the programmer knows which STOP terminated the program.

The last statement in the text of a program (or a program unit, see Chapter 8) must be

END

When encountered, it terminates the execution of the program (or program unit). The END statement cannot be labeled; i.e., no transfer of control is possible to this statement.

In the main program, always precede the END statement with the STOP statement, even through the END statement itself will cause termination.

D. DECISION

A decision construct is used to specify two alternative paths in the program execution. One of these paths is selected during the program execution in accordance with the truth or falsity of the condition stated in the decision. By nesting decision constructs within one another, a choice can be made among several execution paths.

▷ In FORTRAN 77, a powerful tool for implementing general decision constructs is block IF (IF-THEN-ELSEIF-ELSE-ENDIF). In the absence of this mechanism, the logical IF statement is used to implement decisions. ◁

Additional FORTRAN statements that may serve to implement decision and **case** constructs are presented in Section G.

1. GENERAL FORM OF THE DECISION CONSTRUCT

When two alternative execution paths are to be specified in a program, a decision construct is used. It allows the programmer to present the statements to be executed in either case and the condition that has to be tested for the selection. The flowchart symbol for the construct is shown in Fig. 7–2.

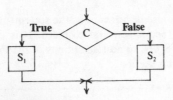

FIGURE 7–2.   Decision construct

This construct may be described in pseudocode as follows:

if the condition C is true **then**
    statement(s) S_1 shall be executed
else
    statement(s) S_2 shall be executed

EXAMPLE 7–3
The selection of the larger of two numbers NUM1 and NUM2 is presented in pseudocode as:

if NUM1 > NUM2 **then**
    MAX ← NUM1
else
    MAX ← NUM2

If the decision involves either executing certain statements or doing nothing (again, depending on a condition), the flowchart of Fig. 7–3 results.

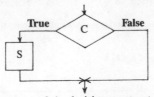

FIGURE 7–3.   A special case of the decision construct

EXAMPLE 7–4

To obtain the absolute value of a number NUM, we may use the following construct:

if NUM < 0 **then**
    NUM $\leftarrow$ $-$NUM
else;

The decisions may also be nested; i.e., the statements S_1 and/or S_2 may be decision constructs themselves, and so forth. It is convenient, while programming in FORTRAN, to nest conditions in the **False** branch, as will be discussed below in this section.

Too "deep" a nesting should be avoided, as it makes programs difficult to read. Try not to nest beyond the level of 3.

---

2. CONDITIONS

To express conditions we use logical expressions, whose value is either **True** or **False**. A simple condition is a relation: two arithmetic expressions connected by a relational operator. In some cases, the arithmetic expression may be simply a constant or a variable.

Relational operators are specified in FORTRAN as shown in Table 7–1.

TABLE 7–1. FORTRAN relational operators. Note that a relational operator is surrounded by periods.

RELATION	ALGEBRAIC NOTATION	FORTRAN
less than	$<$	.LT.
less than or equal to	$\leqslant$	.LE.
equal to	$=$	.EQ.
not equal to	$\neq$	.NE.
greater than or equal to	$\geqslant$	.GE.
greater than	$>$	.GT.

Never test real values that include some obtained through a computation for equality. Since their representations in the computer are only approximations, the actual equality may never occur. Test for their difference being as small as you desire.

EXAMPLE 7-5

(a) The following test on integer variables L, M, and N:

L**2-4 * M * N .EQ. 0

checks whether

$l^2 - 4mn = 0$

(b)To test whether two real variables X and Y have close enough values to be considered equal, we may use this condition:

X - Y .LE. 0.000001

When a more complex condition is to be expressed, relations may be joined by logical operators .OR. or .AND. . A unary logical operator .NOT. may also be applied to a relation. The truth table for these operators is shown as Table 7-2,

TABLE 7-2. Truth table for logical operators, where P and Q are relations

VALUES OF RELATIONS		RESULT OF OPERATION		
P	Q	.NOT. P	P .AND. Q	P .OR. Q
.FALSE.	.FALSE.	.TRUE.	.FALSE.	.FALSE.
.FALSE.	.TRUE.	.TRUE.	.FALSE.	.TRUE.
.TRUE.	.FALSE.	.FALSE.	.FALSE.	.TRUE.
.TRUE.	.TRUE.	.FALSE.	.TRUE.	.TRUE.

The logical constants (.TRUE. and .FALSE. , according to FORTRAN notation) are further discussed in Chapter 9 C.

▷ FORTRAN 77 allows for the use of two additional logical operators, .EQV. and .NEQV. , the first of which corresponds to logical equivalence and the second to exclusive-or operations. ◁

It is easy to think of the three basic logical operators as follows:

.NOT. inverts the value of a relation. If the value is .TRUE. , it becomes .FALSE. and vice-versa.

The condition whose two relations are joined by .OR. is .TRUE. if either of the relations is .TRUE. .

The condition whose two relations are joined by .AND. is .TRUE. only if both relations are .TRUE. .

Thus, a compound condition may be any logical expression that evaluates to .TRUE. or .FALSE. The rules of precedence in this evaluation are the following.

(1) arithmetic operations in the following order:
     exponentiation (**);
     multiplication (*) and division (/);
     addition (+) and subtraction (−);
(2) relational operators (all of equal precedence);
(3) logical operators in the following order:

     .NOT.

     .AND.

     .OR.

Parentheses may be used to change this order of precedence; operations of equal precedence are performed from left to right.

Parenthesize not only when in doubt, but also to make the condition easier to understand.

EXAMPLE 7–6

(a) To encode the following:

> both K and L are negative while M is not positive,

the following condition may be used

    (K .LT. 0) .AND. (L .LT. 0) .AND. (M .LE. 0)

Notes

1. This is more readable than the equivalent:

       K .LT. 0 .AND. L .LT. 0 .AND. M .LE. 0

2. A frequent error is to write

       K .AND. L .LT. 0.

You can avoid such errors if you remember that the logical operators apply only to logical values, while K and L are numerical.

(b) To encode

> the square root of A is greater than 5 while B lies between 10 and 15 exclusively

we may write

    (SQRT(A) .GT. 5.) .AND. (B .GT. 10. .AND. B .LT. 15.)

Note that the numerical intrinsic functions may, of course, be used in a logical expression.

3. BLOCK IF AS A DECISION CONSTRUCT IN FORTRAN 77

One of the major distinctions of FORTRAN 77 in comparison with FOR-
TRAN IV is the block IF mechanism, which allows for a general and readable design of decision constructs.

> Make sure that your system includes this feature; otherwise use the alterna-
> tives presented in the next section.

To implement the flowchart of Fig. 7–2, the following block IF structure
is used:

```
IF (condition) THEN
     statement(s) to be executed if the condition is True
ELSE
     statement(s) to be executed if the condition is False
ENDIF
```

This construct is executed as follows:

(1) The condition is evaluated.
(2) If the value obtained is .TRUE., *only* the statements between the
    THEN and ELSE keywords are executed; otherwise the statements
    following ELSE are executed. Thus, only one group of statements is
    selected for execution.
(3) After the execution of either group of statements, control passes to
    the statement following ENDIF.

The following rules are to be observed.

(1) The ELSE statement (optional, as will be explained below) has to ap-
    pear as the only word in its line.
(2) The ENDIF statement, also the only word in its line, delimits the en-
    tire construct.
(3) No control transfers (for example, through a GOTO) are allowed
    into the block IF construct. (Only transfers to the IF statement itself
    or to the ENDIF are legal.)

> (4) The statements in the THEN and in the ELSE clauses are to be indented
>   for readability by the same number of spaces; for example, five (see the
>   example below).

EXAMPLE 7-7

The following is a part of a larger tax computation problem. A certain income-related tax is paid at a percentage rate (RATE1) on income up to a certain sum (LEVEL) and at a different rate (RATE2) above this sum. The tax value is to be computed for a given taxpayer; the number of taxpayers whose incomes are, respectively, smaller and greater than LEVEL is to be counted.

Since these magnitudes are likely to be changed from year to year, RATE1, RATE2, and LEVEL are variables.

The following pseudocode fragment (presumably incorporated in a larger program) expresses the logic of the solution.

```
*THE TAX RATE ON INCOME BELOW LEVEL IS RATE1, ABOVE
*LEVEL: RATE2
Real INCOME, TAX, LEVEL, RATE1, RATE2, FIXED;
Integer LOW, HIGH;
LOW ← 0; HIGH ← 0; *TAXPAYER COUNTS*
        .
        .
        .
FIXED ← LEVEL * RATE1/100;
        .
        .
        .
if INCOME ≤ LEVEL then
   begin
        TAX ← INCOME * RATE1/100;
        LOW ← LOW + 1
   end
else
   begin
        TAX ← FIXED + (INCOME − LEVEL) * RATE2/100;
        HIGH ← HIGH +1
   end
        .
        .
        .
```

In FORTRAN 77 code we have

```
REAL INCOME, TAX, LEVEL, RATE1, RATE2, FIXED
INTEGER LOW, HIGH
LOW = 0
HIGH = 0
        .
        .
        .
FIXED = LEVEL * RATE1/100.
        .
        .
        .
```

```
IF (INCOME .LE. LEVEL) THEN
        TAX = INCOME * RATE1/100.
        LOW = LOW + 1
ELSE
        TAX = FIXED + (INCOME - LEVEL) * RATE2/100.
        HIGH = HIGH + 1
ENDIF
```

Note that if an edit description F?.2 is used to output the value of the tax, the value will be printed rounded off to the closest cent.

In financial computations, most often this rounded value in dollars and cents has to be obtained (and not only printed as such). This may be accomplished as follows:

```
TAX = FLOAT (IFIX ((TAX + 0.005) * 100.))/100.
```

Analyze it.

Among the statements to be executed in either branch of a block IF there may, naturally, be other block IF constructs.

The ELSE clause in the block IF construct is optional. To implement the flowchart of Fig. 7–3 we use

```
IF (condition) THEN
    statements to be executed if the condition is True
ENDIF
```

If the condition is false, this block IF causes no statements to be executed.

If several different conditions have to be tested (rather than two mutually exclusive conditions), a nested IF - THEN - ELSEIF - ELSE structure is used. The nesting may occur only in the ELSE clause as shown in the flowchart of Fig. 7–4.

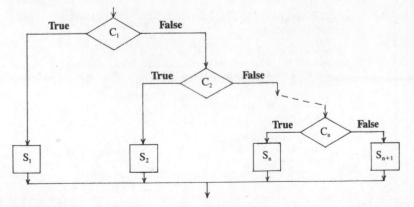

FIGURE 7–4. Nested IF - THEN - ELSE construct

This is accomplished with the use of the following construct.

```
IF (condition - 1) THEN
        S₁
ELSEIF (condition - 2) THEN
        S₂
        .
        .
        .
ELSEIF (condition - n) THEN
        Sₙ
ELSE
        Sₙ₊₁
ENDIF
```

During the execution of this construct, the conditions are tested from top to bottom; when the first condition i whose value is .TRUE. is encountered, S_i is (are) executed and control passes to the statement following ENDIF.

If no condition is .TRUE., the statement(s) S_{n+1} following ELSE is (are) executed. Here also the ELSE clause may be omitted. Thus if no condition is found .TRUE., no statement will be executed.

In keeping with the free use of blanks in FORTRAN, ELSEIF and ENDIF may be written as ELSE IF and END IF, respectively.

EXAMPLE 7-8

To compute and classify into four brackets a tax to be paid by individuals, the following self-explanatory block IF construct may be used.

```
        REAL INCOME, TAX
        INTEGER BRACKT
            .
            .
            .
*       INCOME — RELATED TAX IS COMPUTED
        IF (INCOME .LE. 5000.) THEN
                TAX = 0.
                BRACKT = 1
        ELSEIF (INCOME .GT. 5000. .AND. INCOME .LE. 10000.) THEN
                TAX = .10 * (INCOME — 5000.)
                BRACKT = 2
        ELSEIF (INCOME .GT. 10000. .AND. INCOME .LE. 20000.) THEN
                TAX = 50. + .15 * (INCOME — 10000.)
                BRACKT = 3
        ELSE
*       INCOME IS GREATER THAN $20000
                TAX = 200. + .25 * (INCOME — 20000.)
                BRACKT = 4
        ENDIF
```

These good practices are suggested in the use of nested block IF constructs.
(1) The tests should be ordered in a clear fashion: a logically obvious sequence should be followed.
(2) The test most likely to succeed should be placed first. This makes for efficient computation by preventing superfluous testing. If this contradicts (1) in a particular case, decide which is more important: efficiency or readability.
(3) In programs that are to be reused with some regularity, there should be additional tests for bad data (e.g., negative or suspiciously low or high INCOME in the example above).
(4) Be careful about the boundary conditions; for example is it .LT. or .LE. that you want? Otherwise, some data may "slip through" all tests.
(5) Conditions should be written as clearly as possible, with the use of parentheses where helpful.
(6) Make sure that every IF is matched by ENDIF.
(7) Indent the statements within each clause; for example, by five spaces.

The following program illustrates the use of block IF constructs.

EXAMPLE 7-9

Problem

Obtain roots of a quadratic equation.

Pseudocode of the Solution Algorithm

```
*ROOTS OF A QUADRATIC EQUATION: AX² + BX + C = 0
*ARE COMPUTED
begin
    Input A, B, C;
    Output A, B, C;
    if A=0 and B=0 then
      Output "LOOK AT THE COEFFICIENTS"
    else
      if A=0 then
        begin
            X1← −C/B; Output X1
        end
      else
        if C=0 then
          begin
              X1← −B/A; X2← 0; Output X1, X2
          end
        else
          begin
              DISCR← B**2 − 4*A*C;
              if DISCR ≥ 0 then
```

```
        begin
          X1← (−B+√DISCR)/(2*A);
          X2← (−B−√DISCR)/(2*A);
          Output X1, X2
        end
      else
        begin
          XREAL← −B/(2*A);
          XIMAG← √|DISCR|/(2*A);
          X1← (XREAL,+XIMAG):
          X2← (XREAL,−XIMAG);
          Output X1, X2
        end
    end
  end
end
```

The program is encoded with the use of FORTRAN 77 features; it will not run in a FORTRAN IV implementation.

Note the changes introduced in the code as compared to the pseudocode. These aim to avoid duplicating computations and thus to increase the efficiency of the code. Since the pseudocode is a part of documentation, it aids in the program understanding; note that the pseudocode itself is self-commenting: a reader familiar with quadratic equations needs no explanations.

```
      PROGRAM ROOTS
*     AUTHOR:              DATE:

*     ROOTS OF QUADRATIC EQUATION
*          AX**2 − BX + C = 0
*            ARE COMPUTED

*     A,B,C − EQUATION COEFFICIENTS
*     DISCR − DISCRIMINANT OF THE EQUATION

      IMPLICIT REAL (A−Z)
      READ (5,501) A,B,C
  501 FORMAT(3E10.2)
      WRITE(6,502) A,B,C
  502 FORMAT(' A=', E10.2, 2X, 'B=', E10.2, 2X, 'C=', E10.2)

*     CHECK WHETHER EQUATION IS "C=0"
      IF (A.EQ.0 .AND. B.EQ.0.) THEN
           WRITE (6,503)
  503      FORMAT(' LOOK AT THE COEFFICIENTS!')
      ELSEIF (A.EQ.0.) THEN

*     A SINGLE ROOT
           WRITE (6,504) −C / B
  504      FORMAT(' X=', E10.2)

*     THERE ARE TWO ROOTS
      ELSEIF (C.EQ.0.) THEN
           WRITE (6,505) −B / A, 0.
  505      FORMAT(' X1=', E10.2, 5X, 'X2=', E10.2)
```

```
      ELSE
            DISCR = B ** 2 - 4. * A * C
            TWOA = 2. * A
            RTDISC = SQRT(ABS(DISCR)) / TWOA
            BTWOA = -B / TWOA
            IF (DISCR.GE.O.) THEN
*   TWO REAL ROOTS
                  WRITE (6,505) BTWOA + RTDISC, BTWOA - RTDISC
            ELSE
                  WRITE (6,506) BTWOA,RTDISC,BTWOA, -RTDISC
  506             FORMAT(' X1= (', E10.2, ',', E10.2, 'I)', 5X,
     +                   'X2= (', E10.2, ',', E10.2, 'I)')
            ENDIF
      ENDIF
      STOP
      END
```

The printout below corresponds to the case of two complex roots (this is indicated by I following the second component of each coefficient).

```
A=  0.20E+01  B=  0.20E+01  C=  0.20E+01
X1= ( -0.50E+00,  0.87E+00I)    X2= ( -0.50E+00,  -0.87E+00I)
```

4. CONSTRUCTING DECISIONS WITH THE LOGICAL IF STATEMENT

The old FORTRAN standard did not contain the block IF construct; thus it is not available in FORTRAN IV or in such compilers as WATFOR and WATFIV. When these compilers are used, the logical IF statement is employed to implement decision construct. This statement is available, of course, also in FORTRAN 77.

The logical IF statement allows for the conditional execution of a single statement. It has the general form:

IF (condition) contingent statement

where the condition is stated as a logical expression (see Chapter 7–D–2). The contingent statement may be almost any executable statement (most important statements excluded are other IF statements and DO statements).

The logical IF statement is executed as follows.

(1) The condition is evaluated.
(2) If the value of the condition is .TRUE., the contingent statement is executed; otherwise, the next statement in the program text is executed (as if the logical IF statement did not exist).

If the block IF construct is available, as in FORTRAN 77, it is preferred for use as the general decison construct. In this case, the logical IF statement is used infrequently. In the opposite case it constitutes the essential tool for implementing decision constructs.

The following example presents situations in which the logical IF statement is the desired tool.

EXAMPLE 7–10

(a) To implement the flowchart in Fig. 7–5

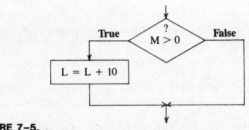

FIGURE 7–5.

we may use the following statement:

```
IF (M .GT. 0) L = L + 10
```

Note that a single logical IF statement suffices for the entire structure.

(b) To keep reading in data until a special trailer card with a value equal to that of a variable NOMORE is encountered, we may use the following loop:

```
10 READ (5,533) ITEM
533     FORMAT(F10.2)
        IF (ITEM .EQ. NOMORE) GOTO 20
        .
        .
    loop body
        .
        .
    GOTO 10
20 ...
```

In the absence of the block IF construct in a given FORTRAN implementation, the logical IF statement is used to design the general decision construct of Fig. 7–2. This is accomplished by placing a GOTO as the contingent statement:

```
        IF (.NOT. (condition)) GOTO label-1

            S₁

            GOTO label-2
label-1 CONTINUE

            S₂

label-2 CONTINUE
```

where S_1 and S_2 represent any number of statements, possibly including other decision constructs.

> If "deep" nesting makes the logic difficult to follow, consider the possibility of using the **case** construct (see Chapter 7–G).

Note that condition C of the flowchart in Fig. 7–2 has to be inverted, so that statement(s) S_1 will be executed when C is .TRUE. and statement(s) S_2 will be executed when C is .FALSE..

The construct presented above should serve as a model that may be modified in actual programming. For example, a simple condition may be inverted without the use of .NOT..

EXAMPLE 7–11
(a) (.NOT. (M .EQ. 0)) is equivalent to (M .NE. 0)
(b) (.NOT. (A .GT. B)) is equivalent to (A .LE. B)

The use of CONTINUE statements is optional and together with indentation (for example, by five spaces) serves to stress the structure.

If a single statement is to be included in either branch, we may code the construct as two statements:

```
IF (condition) S₁
IF (.NOT. (condition)) S₂
```

While the repetition of the condition testing causes a certain inefficiency, this is more readable than its alternative, with two GOTO's.

Note that the following two statements would be incorrect in this case:

```
IF (condition) S₁
S₂
```

since the statement(s) S_2 will be executed regardless of the value of the condition.

EXAMPLE 7-12

The following is a recoding of Example 7–8 with the use of a logical IF:

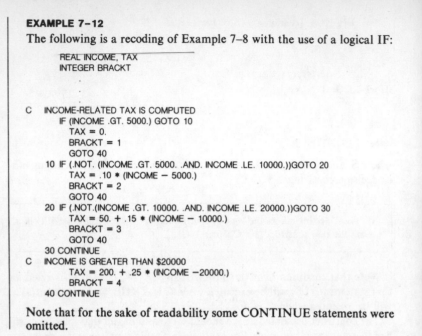

```
      REAL INCOME, TAX
      INTEGER BRACKT
      .
      .
      .
C     INCOME-RELATED TAX IS COMPUTED
      IF (INCOME .GT. 5000.) GOTO 10
      TAX = 0.
      BRACKT = 1
      GOTO 40
10    IF (.NOT. (INCOME .GT. 5000. .AND. INCOME .LE. 10000.))GOTO 20
      TAX = .10 * (INCOME - 5000.)
      BRACKT = 2
      GOTO 40
20    IF (.NOT.(INCOME .GT. 10000. .AND. INCOME .LE. 20000.))GOTO 30
      TAX = 50. + .15 * (INCOME - 10000.)
      BRACKT = 3
      GOTO 40
30    CONTINUE
C     INCOME IS GREATER THAN $20000
      TAX = 200. + .25 * (INCOME -20000.)
      BRACKT = 4
40    CONTINUE
```

Note that for the sake of readability some CONTINUE statements were omitted.

To implement a special case of decision construct without the **else** branch, shown in Fig. 7–3, we may use the following sequence:

```
    IF (.NOT. (condition)) GOTO label

    S

label CONTINUE
```

The need for the construct "if a condition occurs, deal with it, otherwise continue" arises frequently in programming. For example, in a sorting program: "if items are out of order, exchange them," or in handling exceptional situations such as encountering too large a value among the input data: "if this is an exception, deal with it."

EXAMPLE 7-13

To obtain roots of a quadratic equation, the program of Example 7–9 is coded in FORTRAN IV, strictly following the conventions of the old standard. The program will run also in an implementation following FORTRAN 77 standard. Note that the FORTRAN 77 code is shorter and more readable.

```
C    PROGRAM: ROOTS
C    AUTHOR:              DATE:
C
C    ROOTS OF QUADRATIC EQUATION
C          AX**2 - BX + C = 0
C             ARE COMPUTED
C
C    A, B, C - EQUATION COEFFICIENTS
C    X1, X2 - ROOTS OF THE EQUATION
C    DISCR - DISCRIMINANT OF THE EQUATION
C
      IMPLICIT REAL (A-Z)
      READ (5, 501) A, B, C
  501 FORMAT(3E10. 2)
      WRITE (6, 502) A, B, C
  502 FORMAT(3H A=, E10. 2, 2X, 2HB=, E10. 2, 2X, 2HC=, E10. 2)
C
C    CHECK WHETHER THE EQUATION IS "C=0"
      IF (. NOT. (A. EQ. 0. . AND. B. EQ. 0. )) GOTO 10
          WRITE (6, 503)
  503     FORMAT(26H LOOK AT THE COEFFICIENTS!)
          GOTO 50
C
   10 IF (A. NE 0. ) GOTO 20
C
C    A SINGLE ROOT
          X1 = - C / B
          WRITE (6, 504) X1
  504     FORMAT(3H X=, E10. 2)
          GOTO 50
C
C    THERE ARE TWO ROOTS
   20 IF (C. NE. 0. ) GOTO 30
          X1 = - B / A
          X2 = 0.
          WRITE (6, 505) X1, X2
  505     FORMAT(4H X1=, E10. 2, 5X, 3HX2=, E10. 2)
          GOTO 50
   30 CONTINUE
C    GENERAL CASE
          DISCR = B ** 2 - 4. * A * C
          TWOA = 2. * A
          RTDISC = SQRT(ABS(DISCR)) / TWOA
          BTWOA = - B / TWOA
          IF (DISCR . LT. 0. ) GOTO 40
C
C    TWO REAL ROOTS
              X1 = BTWOA + RTDISC
              X2 = BTWOA - RTDISC
              WRITE (6, 505) X1, X2
              GOTO 50
   40     CONTINUE
C
C    TWO COMPLEX ROOTS
          X2IMAG = - RTDISC
          WRITE (6, 506) BTWOA, RTDISC, BTWOA, X2IMAG
  506     FORMAT(6H X1= (, E10. 2, 1H, , E10. 2, 2HI), 5X,
     +           5HX2= (, E10. 2, 1H, , E10. 2, 2HI))
   50 CONTINUE
      STOP
      END
```

CONTROL OF PROGRAM EXECUTION FLOW   115

E. INDEXED (DO) LOOP

A loop allows for a repeated use of a sequence of statements. Such use is called *iteration*. As the statements within the loop are executed, values of certain variables are changed and thus the multiple execution of these statements (which are called loop body) has a cumulative effect.

The looping facility native to FORTRAN, i.e., available as a statement, is the DO statement. It controls a DO loop, which is an indexed loop based on updating the value of the index variable (called also a DO-variable) by a constant number each time the loop is executed and testing the value against a preset limit. If the limit has been exceeded, the iteration is stopped.

The implementation of the more general **while-do** and **repeat-until** loops with the use of logical IF statements is discussed in the next section.

1. GENERAL FORM OF DO STATEMENT

The DO statement provides the facility of the indexed loop. In such a loop, iteration (repeated execution of the loop body) is continued while the index variable, regularly incremented, remains within a preset limit. The DO statement itself maintains the value of the index variable (called also the DO-variable) and checks for the completion of iteration. The general form of the DO statement is

DO   label   DO-variable = initial value, limit, increment

optional

For example,

DO 50 I = LESS, MORE, 10
DO 10 K = 5, 80

The following describes this statement.

(1) The label is attached to the last statement in the loop body. This statement delimits the loop body and thus it cannot precede the DO statement in the program text. This last statement must be an executable statement other than almost any statement controlling execution flow (in particular, it must not be another DO or a GOTO statement).

The range of the DO loop extends from its DO statement through the statement bearing the label referred to. (See box on p. 117.)

(2) The DO-variable controls the iteration. It may not be an array element.

The variable names I, J, K are used most often for integer DO-variables. It is good to reserve them for this purpose.

It is strongly recommended that the last statement in every loop be a CON-TINUE.

By indenting the loop body (e.g., by five spaces) we obtain the following standard form for an indexed loop in FORTRAN, where, again, the increment is optional:

DO   label   DO-variable = initial value, limit, increment

optional

       loop body

  label CONTINUE

For example

```
    DO 10 I = 1, 50, 2
        X = X + 1.
10 CONTINUE
```

(3) If no increment is specified, the default value of 1 is used.

(4) The initial value is assigned to the DO-variable when the loop is entered. Subsequently, every time the last statement in the range of the loop is executed, control is returned to the DO statement. The value of the DO-variable is incremented. If it does not exceed the limit (in the case of a positive increment), the loop body is entered again. If the limit is exceeded, on the other hand, the loop is entered no more and control passes to the statement following it. This execution sequence is presented as a flowchart in Fig. 7–6.

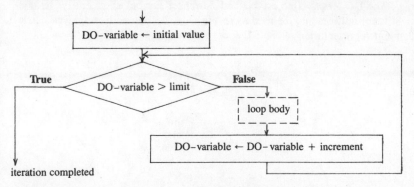

FIGURE 7–6. Flowchart representation of a DO loop in FORTRAN 77 and certain FORTRAN IV systems for a positive increment

▷ Many FORTRAN IV compilers cause the test to be performed *after* the loop body and after the incrementing of the DO-variable (at the point marked X in Fig. 7–6), rather than before the body (see the next section). ◁

(5) No assignment may be made to the DO-variable within the range of the loop. Its value is defined exclusively by the iteration process.

The values of the limit and the increment, once determined when the loop is entered, do not change.

▷ In FORTRAN IV, a DO-variable must be of integer type. Correspondingly, its initial value, limit, and increment may be exclusively integer constants or variables; their value must be greater than 0. Also, the first statement following the DO statement must be executable.

In FORTRAN 77, the DO-variable may be of integer, real, or double precision type. Correspondingly, so may be its initial value, limit, and increment. If the type of these differs from the type of the DO-variable, they are converted to its type. Moreover, any of these three values may be represented by an expression.

The initial value and the limit may be positive, negative, or 0. The value of increment may be positive or negative. In the case of a negative increment, the condition of the decision statement shown in Fig. 7–6 is inverted to read

$$DO\text{-variable} < \text{limit}$$

FORTRAN 77 also permits as an option the use of a comma between the label and the DO-variable in a DO statement.

The differences between the old and the new standards are further discussed in the next section. ◁

The DO loop has no established flowchart symbol as an entity. Its constituent outlines may be used as in Fig. 7–6. A frequently employed convenient representation of the DO loop is shown in Fig. 7–7.

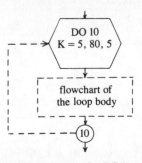

FIGURE 7–7. A convenient representation of a DO loop: DO 10 K = 5, 80, 5

The value of the DO-variable may be used within the loop, as in Example 7–14 below, or serve only as a counter, as in Example 7–15.

EXAMPLE 7–14

The following loop may be used to obtain the sum INTSUM of the first K integers:

```
    INTSUM = 0
    DO 10 I = 1, K
      INTSUM = INTSUM + I
10 CONTINUE
```

Note that a well-known formula for the sum of the arithmetic progression may have been used instead.

EXAMPLE 7–15

The following program computes the average of a set of real numbers that are obtained as input data.

```
C     PROGRAM: MEAN
C     AUTHOR:            DATE:
C
C     MEAN VALUE OF A SET OF REAL NUMBERS IS COMPUTED
C
C     COUNT - OF NUMBERS TO BE AVERAGED
C     VALUE - OF THE REAL NUMBER BEING READ IN
C     SUM   - OF ALL REAL NUMBERS READ
C     AVER  - MEAN (AVERAGE) VALUE
C
      INTEGER COUNT
      REAL VALUE, AVER, SUM
C     HOW MANY NUMBERS ARE TO BE PROCESSED?
      READ (5, 501) COUNT
  501 FORMAT(I10)
C     IS THERE ANY INPUT?
      IF (COUNT .EQ. 0) GOTO 20
C     COMPUTE THE MEAN
          SUM = 0.
          DO 10 I = 1, COUNT
              READ (5, 502) VALUE
  502         FORMAT(F10.2)
              WRITE (6, 503) VALUE
  503         FORMAT(1X, F10.2)
              SUM = SUM + VALUE
   10     CONTINUE
          AVER = SUM / FLOAT(COUNT)
          WRITE (6, 504) AVER
  504     FORMAT(' THE MEAN VALUE IS', F10.2)
          GOTO 30
C
C   THERE IS NO INPUT
   20 WRITE (6, 505)
  505 FORMAT('     NO INPUT DATA')
   30 STOP
      END
```

A sample output is shown below.

```
                    22. 10
                    13. 40
                    55. 10
                    17. 30
                    47. 60
        THE MEAN VALUE IS        31. 10
```

Notes
1. It is assumed that the input data are not to be stored, since no further processing is required. If, on the other hand, we needed to place the data in memory, an array would be used. All the input data are, however, echoed (printed out), which is helpful in debugging.
2. The program is robust: it prints a special message if the count of input data is 0. In many instances it is important to thus provide for special cases.

A DO loop is particularly suitable for processing of arrays; as a matter of fact, such processing is the essential rationale of DO loops. This is illustrated by Example 7–16 and Examples 7–25 and 7–26, of nested loops.

EXAMPLE 7–16
To determine the value and the ordinal number of the largest element in a real array ARR consisting of K elements, we may use the following code fragment:

```
C       TOP IS THE VALUE OF THE LARGEST ELEMENT OF ARR
C       AND TOPIND ITS POSITION IN THE ARRAY
        IMPLICIT INTEGER (A-Z)
        TOP = ARR(1)
        TOPIND = 1
        DO 20 I = 2, K
            IF (ARR(I) .LE. TOP) GOTO 10
            TOP = ARR(I)
            TOPIND = I
10      CONTINUE
20 CONTINUE
```

For efficiency's sake, it is advisable to perform all the loop-invariant computations (i.e., those not influenced by the loop) outside of the loop. The clarity of the code should not be sacrificed for a trivial efficiency gain, however (and, in many cases, the compiler removes the invariant computations outside).

EXAMPLE 7–17
This code fragment

```
    DO 10 I = 1, K
        ITEMS(I) = (5 * MARKS - LOAN) * I
10 CONTINUE
```

should be coded for efficient execution as

```
      NOTES = 5 * MARKS - LOAN
      DO 10 I = 1, K
         ITEMS(I) = NOTES * I
   10 CONTINUE
```

All temporary variables should, if possible, be meaningful in terms of the problem.

Example 7–18 further illustrates the use of DO loops.

EXAMPLE 7-18

Problem
Find the value of a polynomial of degree N for a given X.

Solution
Since the degree of a polynomial is the highest power that appears in it, we have

$$P(X) = A_0 + A_1X + A_2X^2 + \ldots + A_{n-1}X^{n-1} + A_nX^n$$

In order to evaluate this polynomial for any X, we have to carry out the following number of multiplications:

$$1 + 2 + 3 + \ldots + (N - 1) + N = N(N-1)/2$$

and N additions.

Since multiplications are time-consuming operations, it is wise to use for the computation the following equivalent representation of a polynomial, called Horner's rule:

$$P(X) = A_0 + X(A_1 + X(A_2 + \ldots + X(A_{n-1} + XA_n) \ldots)$$

Starting our computation with the inner parentheses, we are thus able to obtain a higher power of X from the already obtained lower power. Thus, the computational complexity becomes N multiplications and N additions.

The following program is the implementation of the formula for polynomials of degree 50 or less.

```
C     PROGRAM: POLYNOMIAL
C     AUTHOR:          DATE:
C
C     VALUE OF POLYNOMIAL IN X OF DEGREE UP TO 50
C     IS COMPUTED WITH THE USE OF HORNER'S RULE
C
C     N - DEGREE OF POLYNOMIAL
C     A(I) - COEFFICIENTS OF POLYNOMIAL
C     POLYN - VALUE OF POLYNOMIAL
C
      INTEGER N
      REAL X, A(51)
      READ (5,501) N, X, (A(I), I = 1, N + 1)
  501 FORMAT(I2, F10.2/ (8F10.2))
      WRITE (6,502) X, (A(I), I = 1, N + 1)
```

```
    502 FORMAT(' X=', F10.2/ ' COEFFICIENTS ARE: '/
   +        (12F10.2))
C
C    VALUE OF THE POLYNOMIAL IS COMPUTED
         POLYN = 0.
         DO 10 I = 1, N + 1
             POLYN = POLYN * X + A(N + 2 - I)
    10 CONTINUE
         WRITE (6, 503) POLYN
    503 FORMAT(15X, 'VALUE OF POLYNOMIAL IS', F16.2)
         STOP
         END
```

A sample printout is shown below.

```
X=        2.00
COEFFICIENTS ARE:
    2.05        3.10        1.25        4.12        7.50
                VALUE OF POLYNOMIAL IS              166.21
```

Notes
1. Note how the coefficients of the polynomial are retrieved from the array $A(I)$.
2. The use of expressions as the limits in DO loops is allowed by FORTRAN 77, but not by the old standard. Thus, in FORTRAN IV an additional variable has to be introduced and assigned the value $N + 1$.

2. COMPATIBILITY AND DIFFERENCES BETWEEN FORTRAN 77 AND FORTRAN IV IN THE USE OF DO LOOPS

It is important to note the following similarities and differences between the new and the old FORTRAN standards and to study the corresponding examples of programming techniques.

In FORTRAN IV, the limit of the DO-variable, as presented in the DO statement, has to be greater than its initial value (since only positive increments are permitted). However, a compiler cannot, in general, check for the conformance to this rule, since both the initial value and the limit may be variables and their values may be unknown before program execution.

Thus, most pre-FORTRAN-77 compilers would execute once a loop whose DO-variable limit is smaller than the initial value! One must be careful of this when using such a compiler and check for this condition with a logical IF statement before the DO statement (see Example 7–22).

In FORTRAN 77, a DO statement may result in a so-called inactive loop, which is simply ignored. This happens when:

    increment > 0 and   limit $<$ initial value
or increment < 0 and   limit $>$ initial value

Since FORTRAN 77 allows the use of real and double precision values to control the loop, the number of times the loop is executed (called iteration count) is computed as follows:

integer part of [(limit − initial value + increment)/increment]

If this value is negative, the iteration count is 0 and the loop is inactive.

EXAMPLE 7-19

(a) The loop controlled by

    DO 10 K = 5, 80

will be executed

    $(80 − 5 + 1)/1 = 76$

times.

(b) The following loop, permissible exclusively in FORTRAN 77,

    DO 20 A = 75.5, − 3.5, − 0.5

will be executed

    $(−3.5 − 75.5 − 0.5)/(−0.5) = 159$

times.

In FORTRAN IV, if the loop is completed (i.e., a transfer of control has not occurred out of it), the value of the DO-variable is undefined. In FOR-TRAN 77, it retains the last value assigned to it during the loop execution (see the flowchart of Fig. 7–6).

EXAMPLE 7-20

If the following statements are executed:

    DO 10 I = 1, 5
        J = I
    10 CONTINUE

then, according to the FORTRAN 77 standard, J = 5 while I = 6 (since the DO-variable was incremented and found too large for another iteration, according to the flowchart of Fig. 7–6).

If the program is written for a FORTRAN system implementing the old (FORTRAN IV) standard or if compability with such systems is desired, the following should be observed.

(1) The DO-variable should be of integer type, and its initial value, limit, and increment should be integer constants or variables, all greater than 0.

Necessary conversions may be performed if these limitations on the DO variable are undesirable in a particular program, as illustrated in Example 7–21.

EXAMPLE 7–21

(a) It is desired to have the DO-variable in the range from N which is greater than 1 to 1, with the increment of -1. The following loop may be implemented:

```
        DO 200 I = 1, N
            K = N − I + 1
C   IN THE REMAINING PART OF THE LOOP BODY,
C   K IS USED AS THE LOOP INDEX
            .
            .
            .
    200 CONTINUE
```

(b) It is desired to implement the loop of Example 7–19(b) under the restrictions of the old standard. The following statements accomplish this task:

```
        DO 20 I = 7, 165
            A = (158. − FLOAT(I))/2.
C   IN THE REMAINING PART OF THE LOOP BODY, A
C   IS USED AS THE LOOP INDEX
            .
            .
            .
        20 CONTINUE
```

Note that the initial value of the redefined control variable A is 75.5 and its limit is -3.5. The iteration count remains, as in Example 7–19(b):

$(165 - 7 + 1)/1 = 159$

(c) The limitations on the initial value, limit, and increment to be an integer constant or an unsubscripted variable may be circumvented as shown by this code fragment:

```
    INIT = IFIX(VALUE(I))
    LIMIT = 5 + MORE − LESS
    DO 20 K = INIT, LIMIT
```

(2) The value of the limit should not exceed the initial value. This may be arranged very simply as shown in this example.

EXAMPLE 7–22

To ensure that the initial value of the DO-variable is no greater than its limit, the following may be done:

```
    IF (INIT .GT. LIMIT) GOTO 30
        DO 20 I = INIT, LIMIT
            .
            .
            .
    20      CONTINUE
    30 CONTINUE
```

(3) It must not be assumed that the DO-variable has any meaningful value after the normal completion of a DO loop.

If it is desirable to retain the value of the DO-variable, it may be stored in a different variable. Note that this is accomplished with the use of variable J in Example 7–20. The value thus obtained is the last one actually used in iteration. Thus it differs from the value automatically retained in FORTRAN 77 by the value of the increment.

3. TRANSFER OF CONTROL AND DO LOOPS

The following limitations hold on the transfer of control from and into a DO loop.

(1) It is forbidden to jump (transfer control) into the body of a loop from the outside code. From the outside, only the transfer of control to the DO statement itself is allowed.

(2) It is allowed to exit the loop before its full completion (see Example 7–23 below) by transferring control out of it.

(3) The transfer of control within the range of a DO loop is, of course, allowed.

If the programmer desires to skip the rest of the statements between the given one and the end of the loop body, the transfer should be to the last statement of the loop (CONTINUE, as a matter of style) and *not* to the DO statement (see Example 7–24 below). If the control were transferred to the DO statement, the execution of the loop would be restarted and thus we would have an "infinite loop."

These rules are illustrated in Fig. 7–8.

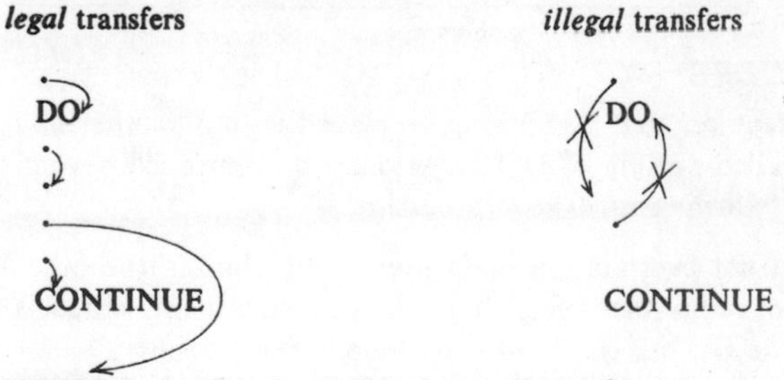

legal transfers   *illegal* transfers

FIGURE 7–8.   Legal and illegal control transfers

The following examples illustrate the use of some legal control transfers.

EXAMPLE 7–23

An array SALARY declared as

```
REAL SALARY(5000)
```

is known to have a single element whose value exceeds 100,000. To find this value and its place in the array (already in memory), the following statements may be used:

```
      DO 10 I = 1, 5000
           IF (SALARY(I) .GT. 100000.) GOTO 20
   10 CONTINUE
   20 WRITE (6,501) SALARY(I), I
  501 FORMAT('THE AMOUNT', F10.2, 'HAS BEEN FOUND IN POSITION ', I4)
```

Note that the loop is exited as soon as the desired item is found.

EXAMPLE 7–24

It is desired to print all the values of the array SALARY of Example 7–23 that exceed 20,000 and their places in the array. The following sequence is used:

```
      DO 30 I = 1, 5000
           IF (SALARY(I) .LE. 20000.) GOTO 20
                WRITE (6,502) SALARY(I), I
  502           FORMAT(1X,F10.2, 5X, I4)
   20      CONTINUE
   30 CONTINUE
```

Avoid control transfers other than to the CONTINUE statement delimiting the loop or to the statement immediately following it (if exit is desired).

---

4. NESTED DO LOOPS

Program logic often requires that a DO loop be placed within another DO loop. This practice, called nesting of DO loops, may be continued beyond the level of two. The following rules govern nesting.

(1) DO loops must not overlap: one loop must fully contain the other one. Nested loops may, however, share the last statement, which is referred to in the DO statement of each loop.

It is recommended that every loop have as a closing statement its own CONTINUE. For readability's sake, the loop body of every loop should be indented, for example, by five spaces.

---

(2) Every DO loop must have its own DO-variable.

(3) The inner loop is fully executed during each iteration of the next-outer loop.

EXAMPLE 7-25

Consider the following nested DO loops:

```
ITER = 0
DO 20 I = 1, N
    DO 10 K = 1, M
        ITER = ITER + 1
10      CONTINUE
20 CONTINUE
```

Here, the outer loop is executed N times while the inner loop is executed N*M times, since it is iterated M times during each of the N iterations of the outer loop. Thus, the value of ITER at the end of the execution equals the value of N*M.

Nested loops are frequently used to manipulate multidimensional arrays, as illustrated by the following example.

EXAMPLE 7-26

This code fragment is self-explanatory.

```
C   ARRAY SALES (I, J) REPRESENTS SALES OF EACH OF THE 50 DISTRICTS
C   IN EVERY ONE OF 30 REGIONS OF A COMPANY
C
        REAL SALES(30, 50), REGSAL(30), TOTAL
        DATA REGSAL/30*0./, TOTAL/0./


C   OBTAIN REGIONAL SALE VOLUMES AND TOTAL VOLUME FOR THE COMPANY
        DO 20 I = 1, 30
C   FOR EVERY REGION
        DO 10 J = 1, 50
            REGSAL(I) = REGSAL(I) + SALES(I, J)
10      CONTINUE
C   FOR THE COMPANY
        TOTAL = TOTAL + REGSAL(I)
20      CONTINUE
```

Study the use of DO-variables in this example.

In the case of nested DO loops, the limitations on the transfer of control explained in the Section F-3 above fully apply. Thus, it is prohibited to jump from an outer loop into an inner one, but it is legal to do the opposite. In an outer loop, it is entirely correct to branch *around* an inner one. These rules apply to any depth of nesting. The rules are illustrated in Fig. 7-9; all the principles shown in Fig. 7-8 also hold.

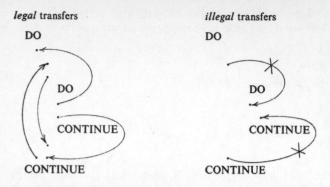

legal transfers   *illegal* transfers

FIGURE 7–9. Legal and illegal control transfers in nested loops.

The following example illustrates nested loops; study the use of the DO-variables in it.

EXAMPLE 7–27 (SELECTION SORT)

Sorting and searching of data are the most common computer applications. There exist, therefore, numerous algorithms to perform these tasks. This is one of simpler sorting algorithms.

Problem

A set of integers is to be sorted. Ascending order is desired: the larger the number, the higher it should stand in the final list.

Solution

The largest number of the set is selected and exchanged with the number with the highest index (i.e., standing in the top place in the list). Subsequently, the largest number of the remaining set is selected and exchanged with the number with the next highest index, etc. For N numbers, this step (pass over the numbers) is repeated $N-1$ times, since the smallest number is automatically placed in the position with the lowest index.

Application of this method to an array of integers is shown below.

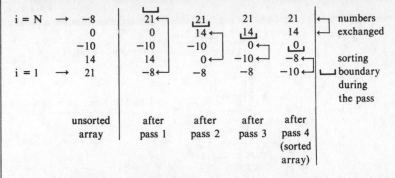

An initial form and a refinement of the selection sort algorithm are presented in Figs. 7–10 and 7–11 (the DO loop symbol of Fig. 7–7 is utilized). The program follows.

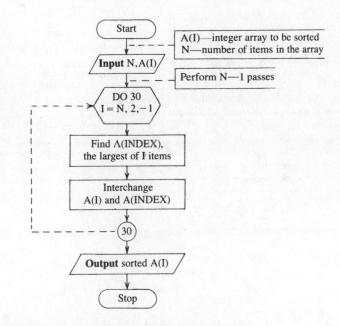

FIGURE 7–10. Initial form of selection sort algorithm

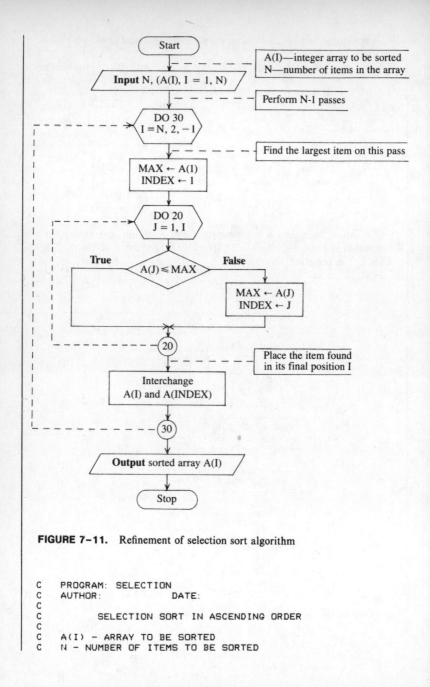

FIGURE 7-11. Refinement of selection sort algorithm

```
C    PROGRAM: SELECTION
C    AUTHOR:            DATE:
C
C         SELECTION SORT IN ASCENDING ORDER
C
C    A(I) - ARRAY TO BE SORTED
C    N - NUMBER OF ITEMS TO BE SORTED
```

```
C     MAX - LARGEST ITEM FOUND DURING THE GIVEN PASS
C     INDEX - POSITION OF THE ABOVE ITEM IN THE ARRAY
C
      IMPLICIT INTEGER  (A-Z)
      DIMENSION A(100)
C   INPUT UNSORTED ARRAY AND ECHO IT
      READ (5,501) N, (A(I), I = 1,N)
  501 FORMAT(I3/ (8I10))
      WRITE (6,502) (A(I), I = 1,N)
  502 FORMAT(10X, 'UNSORTED ARRAY'/ (12X, I10))
C
C   PERFORM  N-1  PASSES OVER THE ITEMS
      DO 30 I = N, 2, -1
C   FIND THE LARGEST ITEM ON THIS PASS
          MAX = A(1)
          INDEX = 1
          DO 20 J = 1, I
              IF (A(J) .LE. MAX) GOTO 10
                  MAX = A(J)
                  INDEX = J
   10         CONTINUE
   20     CONTINUE
C   PLACE THE ITEM FOUND IN ITS FINAL POSITION
          TEMP = A(INDEX)
          A(INDEX) = A(I)
          A(I) = TEMP
   30 CONTINUE
C
C   OUTPUT THE SORTED ARRAY
      WRITE (6,503) (A(I), I = 1,N)
  503 FORMAT(11X, 'SORTED ARRAY'/ (12X, I10))
      STOP
      END
```

A sample output:

```
            UNSORTED ARRAY
                 150
             -123456
                1000
                -400
                  15
                   3
                  24
                   0
              255000
                -500
             SORTED ARRAY
             -123456
                -500
                -400
                   0
                   3
                  15
                  24
                 150
                1000
              255000
```

Notes

1. To grasp better the mechanism of this sorting method, apply it to a set of numbers.
2. Note that we are performing $(N-1)$ passes over the set of numbers, while, on the average, performing $N/2$ comparisons on each pass (close to N at the beginning, close to 1 at the end). Thus, the computational complexity of this sort is on the order of N^2.
3. In one of the DO statements, advantage was taken of a FORTRAN 77 feature: negative increments. If your FORTRAN system does not provide this, Example 7–21(a) shows how to modify the code.

F. GENERAL LOOPS IN FORTRAN

Frequently, an indexed loop such as the DO loop is not adequate to represent the condition for the iterative execution of the loop body.

In most general terms, the programmer often desires that the loop body be executed while a certain condition holds. This is expressed by the **while-do** loop. In other cases, it is more convenient to think of the loop body being repeatedly executed unitl a certain condition arises. This is a **repeat-until** loop.

Both of these constructs may be implemented without difficulty in FORTRAN with the use of the logical IF statement.

1. WHILE-DO LOOP

The flowchart of this construct is shown in Fig. 7–12.

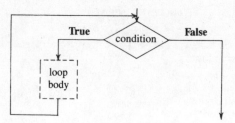

FIGURE 7–12. **while-do** loop. The loop body ultimately changes the value of the condition to **False**.

Note that the loop body is "protected": if the condition does not hold when it is first tested, the loop body is not executed at all. Therefore, this construct is relatively safe in use.

A **while-do** loop may be constructed in FORTRAN as follows with the use of a logical IF statement:

```
10 IF(.NOT.(condition)) GOTO 20
          .
          .
          .
     loop body
     (which will reverse the value of
     the condition)
          .
          .
          .
     GOTO 10
20 CONTINUE
```

To present a condition, a logical expression (see Chapter 7–D–2) is used, as usual in a logical IF statement.

Indent the loop body (for example, by five spaces).

Note that, opposite to a DO loop, the condition will not be reversed automatically here. Thus, unless the programmer provides for its reversal in the loop body, an "infinite loop" may result. This is shown in the following example.

EXAMPLE 7–28

If we wanted to program the loop

```
     DO 10 I = 1, 5
          K = K + I
10 CONTINUE
```

as a **while-do** loop, we would have to provide for the updating of the DO-variable as follows:

```
10 IF(.NOT.(I .LE. 5)) GOTO 20
          K = K + I
          I = I + 1
          GOTO 10
20 CONTINUE
```

or, for the first line:

```
IF(I.GT.5) GOTO 20
```

This example is, of course, an illustration. For a regular updating of a loop control variable by a fixed increment we always use DO loops.

The following example illustrates the use of a **while-do** loop in conjunction with a DO loop.

EXAMPLE 7-29 (ENHANCED BUBBLE SORT)

Problem

As in Example 7-27, a set of integers is to be sorted in ascending order.

Solution

Verbal Description of the Algorithm

A bubble sort consists of a pairwise comparison of adjacent numbers starting at one end of an array of numbers. The pair is exchanged if the numbers are in the opposite order to the desired one. One pass through all the numbers does not, in general, suffice. Passes are repeated until, on the last pass, no exchanges are necessary. This confirms that the numbers are in order.

Application of this algorithm to a sample array of numbers is shown below.

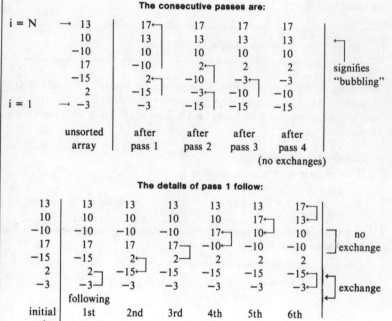

The consecutive passes are:

		unsorted array	after pass 1	after pass 2	after pass 3	after pass 4
$i = N \rightarrow$	13	17	17	17	17
	10	13	13	13	13
	-10	10	10	10	10
	17	-10	2	2	2
	-15	2	-10	-3	-3
	2	-15	-3	-10	-10
$i = 1 \rightarrow$	-3	-3	-15	-15	-15

(no exchanges)

$\leftarrow$ signifies "bubbling"

The details of pass 1 follow:

initial order	following 1st comparison	2nd	3rd	4th	5th	6th
13	13	13	13	13	13	17
10	10	10	10	10	17	13
-10	-10	-10	-10	17	10	10
17	17	17	17	-10	-10	-10
-15	-15	2	2	2	2	2
2	2	-15	-15	-15	-15	-15
-3	-3	-3	-3	-3	-3	-3

no exchange

exchange

Since numbers "bubble up" to take their final place in the array, the algorithm is so named.

It may be observed that the last number moved up during any pass arrives at its final position. An enhanced bubble sort is a bubble sort with a time-saving provision based on this observation: we do not move beyond the number that was moved last at the previous pass. Moreover, if the last number was moved into the position second from "the bottom," the sort has been completed and there is no necessity to make any additional pass without any exchanges.

PSEUDOCODE. INITIAL DESCRIPTION

```
*BUBBLE SORT
begin
    Input array;
    while exchanges are expected do
        perform next pass over the array;
    Output (sorted) array
end
```

PSEUDOCODE. REFINEMENT

```
*ENHANCED BUBBLE SORT IN ASCENDING ORDER
 begin
    Input array;
    mark LIMIT;   *LIMIT—INDEX OF THE LAST ITEM
                            TO BE COMPARED*
*PERFORM CONSECUTIVE PASSES
    while exchanges are expected do
        begin
            start at the bottom;
*PERFORM A SINGLE PASS
            while below LIMIT and LIMIT ≠ 1 do
                begin
                    compare pairwise and exchange
                        if necessary;
                    move to next pair
                end;
            mark new LIMIT
        end;
    Output (sorted) array
end
```

This algorithm is encoded in the following program

```
C    PROGRAM: BUBBLE
C    AUTHOR:              DATE:
C
C            ENHANCED BUBBLE SORT
C              IN ASCENDING ORDER
C
C    A(I) - ARRAY TO BE SORTED
C    N - NUMBER OF ITEMS TO BE SORTED
C    LIMIT - POSITION OF THE LAST ITEM TO BE CONSIDERED
C             DURING THIS SORTING PASS
C    LAST - POSITION OF THE LAST ITEM MOVED DURING THIS PASS
C
        IMPLICIT INTEGER (A-Z)
        DIMENSION A(100)
C    INPUT UNSORTED ARRAY AND ECHO IT
        READ (5,501) N, (A(I), I=1,N)
   501 FORMAT(I3/ (8I10))
        WRITE(6,502) (A(I), I=1,N)
   502 FORMAT(10X, 'UNSORTED ARRAY'/ (12X, I10))
C
C    MARK LIMIT
        LIMIT = N
C    PERFORM CONSECUTIVE PASSES
    10 IF (LIMIT .LE. 1) GOTO 40
        LAST = 0
C    PERFORM A SINGLE PASS
        DO 30 I = 1,LIMIT - 1
C    EXCHANGE THE PAIR IF NECESSARY
               IF (A(I) .LE. A(I+1)) GOTO 20
               TEMP = A(I)
               A(I) = A(I+1)
               A(I+1) = TEMP
               LAST = I
    20         CONTINUE
    30     CONTINUE
C    MARK NEW LIMIT
          LIMIT = LAST
          GOTO 10
    40 CONTINUE
C
C    OUTPUT THE SORTED ARRAY
        WRITE (6,503) (A(I), I = 1,N)
   503 FORMAT(11X, 'SORTED ARRAY'/ (12X, I10))
        STOP
        END
```

A sample output:

```
                UNSORTED ARRAY
                      56789
                        456
                      -1100
                       -125
                       3000
                        -15
                          4
                          0
                         10
                       -500
                      -1000
                      -4000
                    2500000
                     -80000
                  123456000
                 SORTED ARRAY
                     -80000
                      -4000
                      -1100
                      -1000
                       -500
                       -125
                        -15
                          0
                          4
                         10
                        456
                       3000
                      56789
                    2500000
                  123456000
```

2. REPEAT-UNTIL LOOP

Sometimes the loop body has to be executed once before the condition may be tested. This leads to the **repeat-until** loop whose flowchart is shown in Fig. 7–13.

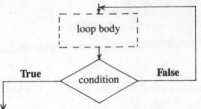

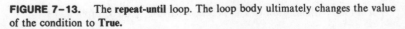

FIGURE 7–13. The **repeat-until** loop. The loop body ultimately changes the value of the condition to **True**.

The FORTRAN implementation of the **repeat-until** loop is

```
10 CONTINUE
     .
     .
     .
     loop body
     (which will reverse the value of
     the condition stated below)
     .
     .
     .
   IF(.NOT.(condition)) GOTO 10
```

Indent the loop body (for example, by five spaces).

A typical situation in which this construct is applicable is shown in the following example.

EXAMPLE 7-30

The values of the elements of a one-dimensional real array WEIGHT are only positive. We do not know the length of the array and thus we will count the number of elements while reading them in. This is accomplished by this code fragment, assuming that the trailer is a negative number:

```
         .
         .
         .
      I = 0
  10  CONTINUE
            I = I + 1
            READ (5,501) WEIGHT(I)
  501       FORMAT(E12.2)
         IF(WEIGHT(I) .GE. 0.) GOTO 10
C  DETERMINE THE ACTUAL LENGTH OF ARRAY
         LENGTH = I - 1
         .
         .
         .
```

Note that the declared dimension of the array has to be 1 longer than its actual length.

For another illustration of the **repeat-until** use, see Example 8–13.

G. COMPUTED GOTO AND MULTIPLE CHOICE

To select one of several execution paths by testing the value of an integer variable (or, in FORTRAN 77, an integer expression in general), a computed GOTO statement may be used. The general form of the computed GOTO statement is

GOTO(label-1, label-2, . . . , label-n), integer expression

For example,

GOTO (40, 20, 10, 20, 30), NUMBER

If the value of the integer expression is between 1 and n, this value determines to which label the execution control is passed.

▷ FORTRAN IV allows exclusively for an unsubscripted integer variable instead of an integer expression. FORTRAN 77 makes the use of the comma after the closing parenthesis optional.   ◁

This statement is executed as follows:

(1) The value of the expression is obtained.
(2) If this value i is such that

$$1 \leqslant i \leqslant n$$

then the next statement executed is the one bearing label-i. If the value of this expression is

$$i < 1 \quad \text{or} \quad i > n$$

then the control passes to the statement following the computed GOTO in the program text.

For example, if the value of the variable NUMBER in the sample statement above is 3, the next statement executed is the one with the label 10.

The computed GOTO statement is used to implement the **case** (multiple choice) construct, used in structured programming to select one of several alternative execution paths. In this construct, control has to pass to a common point from any path. Thus, to implement the construct in FORTRAN, it is necessary to use simple GOTO's as shown in Example 7–31 below.

In most cases, the program logic is more transparent if the labels used by the computed GOTO are placed each on a CONTINUE statement, with every branch being indented (for example, by five spaces).

EXAMPLE 7–31

Problem

The number of adults in various weight categories is to be established (with the view toward printing a bar chart, for example).

The weights range from 81 to 269 lb (all the data supplied are assumed to be correct). The following weight categories are selected:

(1) less than 100 lb;
(2) from 100 to just less than 140 lb;
(3) from 140 to just less than 180 lb;
(4) from 180 to just less than 220 lb;
(5) 220 lb or more.

The data are presented one item per card and delimited by a trailer with a negative number.

Solution

The flowchart is shown in Fig. 7–14 below (the outline selected for the **case** construct is non-standard).

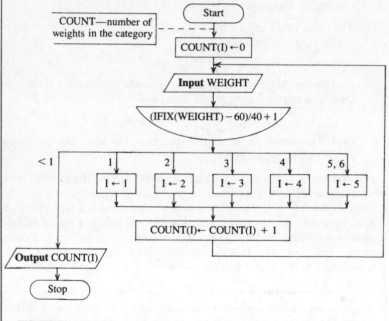

FIGURE 7–14.

The following program is an encoding of this flowchart.

```
C    PROGRAM: WEIGHT
C    AUTHOR:              DATE:
C
C    PROGRAM TALLIES WEIGHTS BY CATEGORIES
C
C    WEIGHT - OF AN ADULT (RANGE: FROM 81 TO 259 LBS)
C    COUNT(1) - NUMBER OF ADULTS WEIGHING LESS THAN 100 LBS
C    COUNT(2) -      "         "        "      FROM 100 TO LESS THAN 140 LBS
C    COUNT(3) -      "         "        "        "   140      "        180 LBS
C    COUNT(4) -      "         "        "        "   180      "        220 LBS
C    COUNT(5) -      "         "        "          220 LBS OR MORE
C
     REAL WEIGHT
     INTEGER COUNT(5)
     DATA COUNT/5*0/
C
C    OBTAIN NEXT WEIGHT
  10 READ (5,501) WEIGHT
 501      FORMAT(F5.1)
C    DETERMINE THE WEIGHT CATEGORY
C
          GOTO (20,30,40,50,60,60) (IFIX(WEIGHT) - 60) / 40 + 1
C
C    LAST CARD REACHED - EXIT
              GOTO 80
  20      CONTINUE
              I = 1
              GOTO 70
  30      CONTINUE
              I = 2
              GOTO 70
  40      CONTINUE
              I = 3
              GOTO 70
  50      CONTINUE
              I = 4
              GOTO 70
  60      CONTINUE
              I = 5
  70      CONTINUE
C
C    TALLY THE WEIGHT
              COUNT(I) = COUNT(I) + 1
C    OBTAIN NEXT WEIGHT
              GOTO 10
  80 CONTINUE
C    OUTPUT RESULTS
     WRITE (6,502) (COUNT(I), I = 1,5)
 502 FORMAT(' LESS THAN 100', 2X, 'FROM 100 TO 140', 2X,
    +       'FROM 140 TO 180', 2X, 'FROM 180 TO 220', 2X,
    +       'MORE THAN 220'/ 4X, 5(I5, 11X))
     STOP
     END
```

This is a sample output:

```
LESS THAN 100  FROM 100 TO 140  FROM 140 TO 180  FROM 180 TO 220  MORE THAN 220
     1               1                1                2                0
```

Notes

1. The same program could be designed with logical IF statements, but the logic would be less transparent (try it!).
2. If a FORTRAN 77 system is not available, the expression used in the computed GOTO has to be assigned to an intermediate variable and used as such.

H. USE OF ARITHMETIC IF STATEMENT

When a threeway branch is desired, an arithmetic IF statement may be used. It has the following general form:

IF (arithmetic expression) label-1, label-2, label-3

where the expression may be of integer, real, or double precision type. For example,

IF (2 * J − M) 10, 20, 10

This statement is evaluated as follows:

(1) The arithmetic expression is evaluated.
(2) If the value of the expression is negative, control is transferred to the statement bearing label-1; if this value is 0, control goes to the statement with the label-2; if the value is positive, to label-3.

All three target statements have to be executable, but not necessarily distinct. For example, the statement above tests, in effect, for

2 * J − M .EQ. 0

The (nonstandard) flowchart of the arithmetic IF statement is shown in Fig. 7–15.

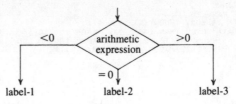

FIGURE 7–15. Arithmetic IF statement

While this statement may be found useful in numerical computations, the programmer should consider using logical IF statements instead. The arithmetic IF tends to obscure the logic of the program.

EXAMPLE 7-32

In a program used to obtain roots of a quadratic equation, the following approach may be used:

```
            .
            .
      IF (B ** 2 - 4. * A * C) 10, 20, 30
    10 CONTINUE
C   COMPLEX ROOTS
            .
            .
            .
        S₁
            .
            .
            .
      GOTO 40
    20 CONTINUE
C   IDENTICAL REAL ROOTS
            .
            .
            .
        S₂
            .
            .
            .
      GOTO 40
    30 CONTINUE
C   DISTINCT REAL ROOTS
            .
            .
            .
        S₃
            .
            .
            .
    40 CONTINUE
```

Note the indentation and the use of CONTINUE statements employed to make this structure more readable.

8

MODULAR PROGRAMMING IN FORTRAN

The programmer needs a facility that serves to break up a program into functionally independent modules, in FORTRAN called program units. Modules communicate by exchanging data. A purposeful program design with such units is called *modular programming*.

Modular programming has the following advantages over straight-line coding of larger programs:

- A modular program is easier to design and implement, particularly if the designer uses the stepwise refinement method.
- A modular program, if well documented, is easier to understand.
- A modular program is easier to modify, since we may deal only with the modules affected by the modification.
- An overall programming effort lends itself to a better organization if more than one programmer is involved.
- Multiple use of tested modules (as an alternative to the code repetition) in a program results in increased program reliability as well as saving of programming effort and memory space.

> While hard-and-fast rules cannot be offered, the length of a program unit should not exceed 50–100 statements.

Program units include the main program (always present) and subprograms. Two essential types of subprograms may accompany the main program: subroutines and (external) functions. These are independent modules with their own names whose code is included along with that of the main program.

A subprogram is executed when it is invoked by the main program or by another subprogram.

Both subroutines and functions may be used to compute any number of values. Good programming practices, however, demand the use of subroutines when several results are to be obtained, and the use of functions when a single value to be assigned to the name of the function is computed.

Two program units communicate either through arguments stated in the argument list of the subprogram being invoked and/or through commonly accessible data. In the case of a function, the invoking program unit also receives data via the function name.

As additional facilities, intrinsic functions (discussed in Chapter 6–C) and statement functions (one-liners included in the code of the program unit where they are used) are available.

To initialize a named block of commonly accessible data, a BLOCK DATA subprogram may be utilized. Its use is rather infrequent.

A. GENERAL DISCUSSION OF FORTRAN PROGRAM UNITS

A FORTRAN program consists of at least a *main program* that always receives control when the program execution is started. In a larger program, functionally separate sequences of statements may be identified. These will be cast into *subprograms*, which are executed only when invoked by the main program or other subprograms. A subprogram, once defined, may be used several times during the program execution.

The main program and the subprograms are called *program units* (see Fig. 8–1 for the classification).

The two most important types of subprograms are subroutines and (external) functions. Subroutine and function subprograms perform their own computations and may return the results to the program unit that invoked them. Subroutine, the most general and useful type of subprogram, may be used to compute any number of values and present them to the invoking program. The invocation of subroutine is termed *subroutine call;* it constitutes a separate statement.

The use of functions is somewhat limited: a function is essentially utilized to obtain a single value, which the function assigns to its own name (although a function may also compute several values). The function name acquires a value as the result of its invocation; thus no separate call is required to the function. The function name may be simply used in place of a variable of the same type; we then speak of *function reference.*

For simplicity's sake, we sometimes speak of both subroutines and functions being "called." After its execution has been completed, a subroutine or a function returns control to the place of call; this is the *return* from a subprogram.

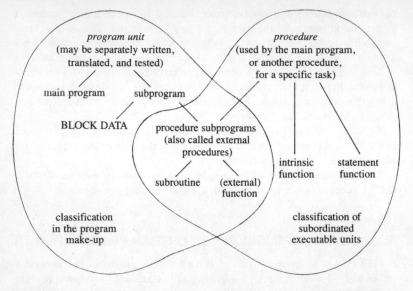

FIGURE 8–1. Classification of program units and procedures in FORTRAN

Since a subroutine or a function is called upon to perform a computation, it most often needs to acquire certain data from the invoking program unit and to pass certain results back to it. Such communication between program units occurs either by passing of *arguments* or by sharing common data. In the case of a function, a single result is passed back as the value of the function name.

Including a procedure subprogram in a program involves three actions.

- It has to be defined, i.e., programmed.
- It has to be invoked, i.e., used.
- The provision has to be made for passing the data, if necessary, to and from it.

Subprograms are placed immediately after the main program in a FORTRAN job. Thus, the "program statements," presented as a component of a FORTRAN job in Chapter 3–C–1, are expanded as shown:

```
control cards
[main program]
[subprogram-1]
        .
        .
        .
[subprogram-N]
```

control card(s) to delimit program from data
.
.
.

Thus, the subprograms are placed after the main program.

▷ In FORTRAN 77, the main program may also begin with a PROGRAM statement of the general form:

PROGRAM name

where "name" is a symbolic name (of up to six alphanumeric characters beginning with a letter). This name is assigned to the main program and may not be used in it for any other purpose. ◁

Subprograms begin depending on their nature, with a SUBROUTINE, FUNCTION, or BLOCK DATA statement (described further in this chapter). Thus, the main program may be distinguished by not beginning with either of these. Every program unit ends with an END statement.

Subprograms may be placed in any order, following the main program. Subroutines and functions are executed exclusively as the result of their invocations; following its execution, a subprogram returns control to the place of the invocation. A BLOCK DATA subprogram is not executable; it is used to assign initial values to data items in named common blocks during the translation of the program.

EXAMPLE 8–1

A certain program consists of a main program and two subroutines—SORT, which sorts an array in ascending order, and EXCHANGE, which exchanges the values of two variables. The hypothetical order of invocations is illustrated in Fig. 8–2.

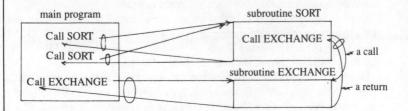

FIGURE 8–2.   Here ○ indicates a corresponding call and return.

Note the various possibilities of invocations.

In the job make-up, it does not matter whether the subroutine SORT precedes EXCHANGE or vice-versa.

The dependence between program units in a particular program may be presented in a *structure chart,* which shows which subprograms are invoked by which program units. A structure chart is accompanied by an *interface table,* which specifies the data passed between the program units, through the interfaces between the units, as it were. (See Table 8–3 on p. 180.)

Example 8–1 will be represented as follows:

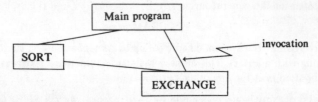

FIGURE 8–3.   A structure chart

FORTRAN prohibits recursive calls: a subprogram may not invoke itself. Neither is it possible for a subprogram to invoke itself indirectly, through intermediate subprograms.

Every subprogram is an independent program unit, with its own data declarations, if needed. This means that all the variable and array names and all labels used in a program unit are local to it: these names are not known in other program units. Therefore, the same names and labels may be used in several units. Thanks to this, the program units may be coded independently.

During the use of subroutines and functions, values may be assigned to variables or array elements of the invoked subprogram by the invoking program unit. Conversely, a subroutine may assign values to variables or array elements named in the call as actual arguments. Data may also be passed through variables and arrays placed in common blocks. This is what is meant by communication between program units.

Subroutines and external functions are the essential *procedures* (invoked instruction sequences performing specific tasks) available in FORTRAN. Aside from these, two other kinds of procedures exist in FORTRAN (see Fig. 8–1): intrinsic functions and statement functions.

Intrinsic functions are built into the language itself; i.e., they are provided as part of the translator for the language and do not have to be defined by the programmer who uses them. Their use is described in Chapter 6–C, and some of them are mentioned in other of the books chapters, which deal with the subject matter to which these functions pertain (e.g., character processing in Chapter 9).

Statement functions are one-line statements embedded in program units and thus not independent program units themselves (see Section H of this chapter).

B. SUBROUTINES

The subroutine is the most general type of subprogram: it may serve to calculate any number of results.

The program unit that calls a subroutine may communicate data to it as the values of actual arguments or through common blocks, discussed in Section D of this chapter. After the subroutine has been executed, the results are passed back to the calling program unit, also through the arguments or common blocks.

1. HOW TO DEFINE A SUBROUTINE

A subroutine is a separate program unit composed of the SUBROUTINE statement followed by the body of the subroutine and terminated by the END statement.

A subroutine definition has thus the following general form:

SUBROUTINE subroutine name(list of dummy arguments)
.
.
.
statements of the subroutine
.
.
.
RETURN
END

A subroutine name is formed, like any FORTRAN symbolic name, of up to six alphanumerical characters, the first one being a letter. It has no type, since no value may be assigned to it.

The list of dummy arguments specifies the names by which the data items passed by the calling program and/or to be passed to it are known in the subroutine. Thus, these are essentially variable or array names. *Dummy arguments* are place-holders for the *actual arguments* supplied by the calling unit. Argument passing is discussed in detail in Section B–3.

If no arguments are to be passed, this list is absent. Thus two general forms of the SUBROUTINE statement exist:

SUBROUTINE subroutine name(argument-1, . . . , argument-n)
or   SUBROUTINE subroutine name

For example

SUBROUTINE FIND(ARR, ELMNT)
or   SUBROUTINE OBTAIN

Since a subroutine is an independent program unit, all variable and array names used in it are local: they are not known in other units of the program.

Thus, their type must be specified explicitly or implicitly in the subroutine itself (according to the rules presented in Chapter 4–B). The dimensions of the arrays used by a subroutine must also be declared in it (see Chapter 6–A). In the case of arrays which are arguments, variable dimensions may be specified and their values passed to the subroutine as arguments, as discussed further in this section.

Variables and/or arrays used in a subroutine may be

- dummy arguments
- parts of common blocks shared with other program units
- or local entities, which exist exclusively in the subroutine.†

The labels used in a subroutine are local; the same labels may be used in other program units.

The execution of a RETURN statement causes the return of control to the calling program unit. Thus, this statement is used to stop the subroutine execution.

A subroutine may contain more than one RETURN statement if its logic so requires, which is analogous to the main program having more than one STOP statement.

The END statement delimits the subroutine.

▷ FORTRAN 77 does not require a RETURN statement before END; the old standard does, however. It is a good practice to include the RETURN statement. ◁

2. HOW TO USE (CALL) A SUBROUTINE

To use a subroutine, i.e., to cause its execution, a CALL statement has to be included in the calling program unit. The general form of the CALL statement is

CALL subroutine name(list of actual arguments)

Corresponding to the SUBROUTINE statement of the invoked subroutine, the argument list may be absent; for example,

```
CALL FIND(SET, MEMBER)
CALL OBTAIN
```

This executable statement may be placed anywhere in the calling unit where other executable statements may be placed.

Since one of the goals of writing subroutines is their multiple use, naturally several CALL's to the same subroutine may be contained in a given

---

†The values of these local variables and arrays are not, in general, saved between the invocations of a subroutine (although some implementations may save them).

program unit or other program units of the program, with the exception of the given subroutine itself.

The actual arguments listed in the CALL statement must correspond in number and type to the dummy arguments listed in the corresponding SUBROUTINE statement. This has to be so because the actual and dummy arguments are associated with one another by their positional correspondence: the first actual argument with the first dummy argument, etc. The actual and the dummy argument in the same position in their respective lists refer to the same entity (a variable or an array).

EXAMPLE 8-2

The following illustrates the association of arguments in CALL statements with those in SUBROUTINE statements. We assume that these statements are contained in a certain program:

REAL SET(100), MEMBER
.
.
.

CALL   FIND(SET, MEMBER)

            a real   a real
            array   variable

SUBROUTINE FIND(ARR, ELMNT)
REAL ARR(100), ELMNT
.
.
.

Dummy arguments are the names used in the subroutine for the entities (such as variables and arrays) whose values are passed to the subroutine by the calling unit or vice-versa. The *actual arguments* are the values passed to the subroutine (which may have to be obtained when the CALL is executed) or the names used for entities to be evaluated by the subroutine. Sometimes, an actual argument serves both purposes. To understand better argument passing, read Section B-3.

Be very careful that the list of actual arguments in the CALL to a subroutine matches the list of dummy arguments in its SUBROUTINE statement. A mismatch of the two is a very frequent error. A tool that helps ensure that these two lists match is the interface table of the program, which should accompany its structure chart (as will be seen in Example 8-20).

In certain cases, it is advantageous to communicate with a subroutine through a common block along with or instead of an argument list (see Section D of this chapter).

The following sequence of events occurs when a subroutine is called:

(1) All expressions contained in the actual argument list are evaluated, and thus all available values of actual arguments are obtained.

(2) The actual arguments stated in the CALL are associated with the dummy arguments listed in the SUBROUTINE statement, as discussed in the next section.

(3) The subroutine is executed.

(4) When a RETURN (or, in its absence, the END) statement is encountered during the subroutine execution, control returns to the statement following the CALL in the invoking program unit.

All the values that have been assigned by the subroutine to the dummy parameters that correspond to such actual parameters as variables, array elements, or arrays, are available to the invoking unit.

Subroutine call is illustrated with the following trivial example.

EXAMPLE 8-3

```
C    SERIES OF DIFFERENCES OF TWO INTEGERS IS OBTAINED
C
         IMPLICIT INTEGER (A-Z)
      10 READ (5,501, END = 20) INT1, INT2
     501     FORMAT(2I10)
             CALL SUBTR(INT1, INT2, DIFF)
             WRITE (6,502) INT1, INT2, DIFF
     502     FORMAT(3(5X, I10))
         GOTO 10
      20 STOP
         END
C
C    DIFFERENCE OF TWO INTEGERS IS OBTAINED
C
         SUBROUTINE SUBTR(NUM1, NUM2, MINUS)
C
         IMPLICIT INTEGER (A-Z)
         MINUS = NUM1 - NUM2
         RETURN
         END
```

The subroutine SUBTR obtains the values of INT1 and INT2 from the main program and passes back to it the value of MINUS, known in that program unit as DIFF.

In a flowchart, subroutine calls are shown as in Fig. 8–4.

FIGURE 8–4. A flowchart outline of a subroutine call

A subroutine itself is flowcharted as an independent program unit. An annotation outline (see Chapter 2) may be used to specify the actual arguments in the call and the dummy arguments in the subroutine as shown in Fig. 8–5. The arguments, if few, may also be placed in the call outline itself.

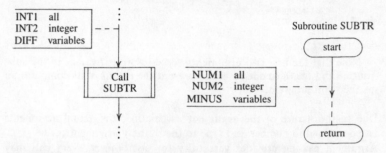

FIGURE 8–5. Use of annotation outlines to specify arguments

3. HOW ARGUMENTS ARE PASSED

During a subroutine call, the actual arguments listed in the CALL statement are associated with the dummy arguments listed in the SUBROUTINE statement that heads the subroutine called. Through this association, data may be passed to the subroutine from the calling program unit and vice-versa.

The association means that the dummy arguments acquire the values possessed by their corresponding actual arguments at the time of the call.† In turn, when the return from the subroutine occurs, the actual arguments referring to variables, array elements, or arrays may acquire values assigned to their corresponding dummy arguments in the subroutine.

---

†Actually, in FORTRAN implementations, argument passing is most frequently performed by reference. Thus, if the actual argument is a single value, its address is passed to the subroutine. If the actual argument is an array, the address of its first element is passed.

The association between the actual and dummy arguments is made by their positional correspondence. This means that if the calling statement

refers to

CALL   ANYSUB (ACT1, ACT2, ACT3)
$\updownarrow$ $\updownarrow$ $\updownarrow$
SUBROUTINE ANYSUB (DUM1, DUM2, DUM3)

then the shown association occurs.

This is illustrated by the following extremely simplified example.

EXAMPLE 8–4

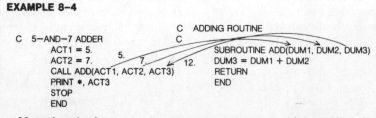

```
C  5-AND-7 ADDER              C  ADDING ROUTINE
     ACT1 = 5.                C
     ACT2 = 7.                   SUBROUTINE ADD(DUM1, DUM2, DUM3)
     CALL ADD(ACT1, ACT2, ACT3) DUM3 = DUM1 + DUM2
     PRINT *, ACT3              RETURN
     STOP                       END
     END
```

Note that the first two arguments serve to present values to the subroutine and the third one serves to present the results of its computation to the main program.

Due to the nature of the argument association, the actual arguments must correspond in number and type to the dummy arguments.

Argument passing provides versatility for subroutines; every call may present its own actual arguments as shown in the example below.

EXAMPLE 8–5

Observe these two calls to a single subroutine. (Here the circled numbers indicate call-return combinations.)

main program

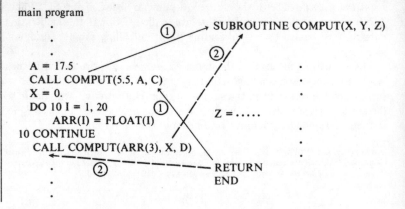

```
      .
      .
      .
   A = 17.5
   CALL COMPUT(5.5, A, C)
   X = 0.
   DO 10 I = 1, 20
        ARR(I) = FLOAT(I)
10 CONTINUE
   CALL COMPUT(ARR(3), X, D)
      .
      .
      .
```

SUBROUTINE COMPUT(X, Y, Z)

Z = ...

RETURN
END

The following occurs during the execution of the presented fragment of the main program:

The subroutine COMPUT is called twice. During the first call, the subroutine acquires the values

$$X = 5.5 \qquad Y = 17.5$$

and through the dummy argument Z assigns a value to the variable C in the main program.

During the second call, the subroutine acquires the values

$$X = 3. \qquad Y = 0.$$

and upon return assigns through the dummy argument Z a value to the variable D in the main program.

Note that since the symbolic names in the main program are independent of the symbolic names in a subroutine, the variable name X used in the subroutine refers to an entirely different location than the same name refers to in the main program. The use of the same name should be regarded simply as a coincidence.

Table 8–1 shows the essential† entities that may appear in the corresponding positions in the two argument lists.

TABLE 8–1. Possible argument list correspondences

ACTUAL ARGUMENTS (in the calling program unit)	DUMMY ARGUMENTS (in the called program unit)
constants } may *not* serve as output arguments	
expressions	
	variables (*only* unsubscripted)
variables	
array elements	
array names	array names
Some subroutines have no arguments at all.	

The following rules apply:

(1) If the actual argument is an expression, it is evaluated immediately before the transfer to the subroutine occurs.

†Also a function or a subroutine name may be passed as an argument. This very infrequently used capability is beyond the scope of our discussion.

(2) If the actual argument is an array element, its subscript (which may be an expression) is evaluated immediately before the transfer to the subroutine. Thus is selected a definite array element that does not change throughout the subroutine execution (but its value may, of course, change).

Some arguments are used to pass data to the subroutine; these are often informally called *input arguments* (see the first two arguments in Example 8–5). Some arguments are used to pass results to the calling program upon the return from the subroutine. These are called *output arguments* (e.g., the third argument in Example 8–5). Sometimes, an argument serves to pass a value to the subroutine during the call and then a result back to the calling program in return.

> It is a good programming practice to avoid "two-way" arguments that pass values in both directions. Strict subdivision into input and output arguments makes for easier testing of subroutines and helps to avoid errors.

Any actual argument that is expected to present a value to a subroutine, must, naturally, acquire it in the calling program before the call.

The dummy arguments corresponding to the actual arguments, which are constants and expressions, may not be used to pass values back to the calling program (what sense would it make to try to assign a new value to a constant?).

The following illustrates a simple use of a subroutine.

EXAMPLE 8–6

Problem

A set of integer numbers is sorted in descending order. We are to reorder it into ascending order.

In other words, assuming that the numbers are placed in the array ITEMS, we have to change this order:

ITEMS (1) $\geqslant$ ITEMS(2) $\geqslant \ldots \geqslant$ ITEMS(N)

to this:

ITEMS (1) $\leqslant$ ITEMS(2) $\leqslant \ldots \leqslant$ ITEMS(N)

Solution

The pseudocode of the solution is

*REORDERING ALGORITHM
begin
    Integer N, ITEMS;
    Input N, ITEMS(1:N);
    I ← 1;
    while I ≤ N/2 **do**
        begin
            Call EXCHGE(ITEMS(I), ITEMS(N−I+1));
            I ← I +1
        end
end
*VALUES OF TWO VARIABLES ARE EXCHANGED
Subroutine EXCHGE(K, L)
begin
    Integer K, L, TEMP;
    TEMP ← K;
    K ← L;
    L ← TEMP
end

A corresponding FORTRAN program follows.

```
C    PROGRAM: INVERT
C    AUTHOR:              DATE:
C
C    A DESCENDING LIST IS REORDERED INTO THE ASCENDING ONE
C
C    ITEMS(I) - ITEMS TO DE REORDERED
C    N - LIST LENGTH
C
     IMPLICIT INTEGER (A-Z)
     DIMENSION ITEMS(100)
     READ (5,501) N, (ITEMS(I), I = 1,N)
 501 FORMAT(I4 / (8I10))
     WRITE (6,502) (ITEMS(I), I= 1,N)
 502 FORMAT(' ORIGINAL LIST' / (2X, I10))
C
C    IF THE NUMBER OF ITEMS IS ODD, THE MIDDLE ITEM STAYS IN PLACE
     DO 10 I = 1,N / 2
        CALL EXCHGE(ITEMS(I),ITEMS(N - I + 1))
  10 CONTINUE
     WRITE (6,503) (ITEMS(I), I = 1,N)
 503 FORMAT(' INVERTED LIST'/ (2X, I10))
     STOP
     END


C
C    VALUES OF TWO INTEGER VARIABLES ARE EXCHANGED
C
     SUBROUTINE EXCHGE(K,L)
C
     IMPLICIT INTEGER (A-Z)
     TEMP = K
     K = L
     L = TEMP
     RETURN
     END
```

A sample printout:

```
        ORIGINAL LIST
            50000
             4555
             2000
              123
               50
                9
                5
                0
              -47
             -300
           -12500
        INVERTED LIST
           -12500
             -300
              -47
                0
                5
                9
               50
              123
             2000
             4555
            50000
```

When an array is passed as an argument, its dimensions have to be declared (e.g., by a DIMENSION or a type statement) in both the calling program unit and in the subroutine. The size of the array that appears as the dummy argument may equal or be smaller than the size of the array which is the actual argument.

EXAMPLE 8-7

This main program:

```
REAL SCORES(100), MEAN, DEV
      .
      .
      .
CALL STAT(SCORES, MEAN, DEV)
      .
      .
```

calls this subroutine:

```
SUBROUTINE STAT(RESLTS, MEAN, DEV)
REAL RESLTS(100), MEAN, DEV
      .
      .
MEAN = ...
DEV = ...
      .
      .
RETURN
END
```

The subroutine, presumably, computes statistical information on a number of scores.

The size of the dummy array RESLTS could be smaller than 100, but not greater.

For multidimensional arrays, use can be made of the fact that the arrays are stored in a column order in memory (as described in Chapter 6–A–4) to "restructure" an array in the subroutine. Such usage leads to difficulty in locating errors and should be avoided. Thus, if fixed array dimensions are declared in both the calling and the called program unit, they should be the same except, possibly, for arrays with a single dimension.

Significant flexibility may be attained in FORTRAN programming through the use of *adjustable dimensions*. An array in a subprogram is said to have adjustable dimensions if the array itself, as well as its dimensions, are passed to the subprogram as arguments. This means that in the subprogram the array is declared with variable dimensions. Thus, the subprogram becomes general enough to manipulate arrays of any size.

The program unit that calls the subprogram using an array with adjustable dimensions (or another unit higher in the chain of calls) needs to specify fixed dimensions for the array that is the actual argument corresponding to the dummy array with adjustable dimensions. Also, the value of dimensions passed should conform to the rule that the size of a dummy array may not exceed the size of the corresponding actual array.

EXAMPLE 8–8

Two matrices may be added if they have the same number of rows and the same number of columns. To add two integer matrices of any size, the following subroutine may be used:

```
C   TWO INTEGER MATRICES, MAT1 AND MAT2, ARE ADDED
C          TO OBTAIN A MATRIX MATRES
      SUBROUTINE MATADD(MAT1, MAT2, MATRES, M, N)
C
      INTEGER MAT1(M, N), MAT2(M, N), MATRES(M, N)
      DO 20 I = 1, M
         DO 10 J = 1, N
            MATRES(I, J) = MAT1(I, J) + MAT2(I, J)
   10    CONTINUE
   20 CONTINUE
      RETURN
      END
```

This subroutine may be called by a program unit containing the following statements:

```
        INTEGER PURCH1(200, 20), PURCH2(200, 20), PURTOT(200, 20),
    +          SALES1(50, 100), SALES2(50, 100), SALTOT(50, 100)



        CALL MATADD(PURCH1, PURCH2, PURTOT, 200, 20)



        CALL MATADD(SALES1, SALES2, SALTOT, 50, 100)
```

The example below illustrates a number of possibilities in argument passing.

EXAMPLE 8–9

The following is a legitimate subroutine call, provided that all the values necessary to compute the input arguments (marked ↓) are assigned before the CALL. Values of the output arguments (marked ↑) will be assigned by the subroutine.

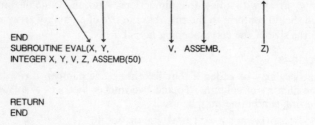

```
    INTEGER HIGH, LOW, COLLCT(50)


    CALL EVAL(5, 3*SQRT(FLOAT(LOW)), LOW, COLLCT, COLLCT(HIGH − LOW))



    END
    SUBROUTINE EVAL(X, Y,           V,  ASSEMB,      Z)
    INTEGER X, Y, V, Z, ASSEMB(50)


    RETURN
    END
```

C. FUNCTIONS

The essential purpose of an external function (or, for short, a function) is to return to the invoking unit a single value that is assigned to the name of the function during its execution. If the function has to compute additional values, it is possible to pass them to the invoking program unit through output arguments or common memory areas, as in the case of subroutines. In these cases, the use of a subroutine instead of a function is advisable, however.

1. HOW TO DEFINE A FUNCTION

A function is a separate program unit composed of a FUNCTION statement, followed by the body of the function, and terminated by an END statement. Thus, a function definition has the following general form

type FUNCTION function name (list of dummy arguments)
 optional   optional

statements of the function, where a value is
. assigned to the name of the function

RETURN
END

Since a value has to be assigned to the function name, this name (unlike practice with a subroutine) has to be of a definite type. Any legal FORTRAN type may be specified or, alternatively (but not both!), the type of the function may be specified in a type statement in the function itself. With integer and real functions, it is also possible to use implicit specifications: if the function name starts with I through N, it is an integer function; otherwise the function is real. The function name is formed like any other symbolic name in FORTRAN.

EXAMPLE 8–10
These are three equivalent ways of specifying a real function:

    REAL FUNCTION WORK(X, M)

or

    FUNCTION WORK(X, M)
    REAL WORK, . . .

or

    FUNCTION WORK(X, M)

The list of dummy arguments specifies the names by which the actual arguments listed in the function reference ("call") are known in the function itself.

▷ Most implementations of FORTRAN IV require that a function have at least one argument, so that a reference to it may be distinguished from a variable.

In FORTRAN 77, a function without arguments is denoted as follows (where type is optional):

    type FUNCTION function name ( )   ◁

The type of all variables and arrays used by the function has to be specified in it, independent of the specifications in other program units. The array dimensions must also be declared; in the case of arrays that are arguments, variable dimensions may be specified and their values passed as arguments (see Section B–3 above). All variable and array names and labels used in a function are local to it.

A value of the appropriate type has to be assigned to the function name before control returns to the program unit that invoked the function.

When a function execution is started, the function name has no value. In the function itself, this name is used simply as a variable name of the same type would be used.

EXAMPLE 8–11

A value may be assigned to an integer function BUSY as follows:

```
INTEGER FUNCTION BUSY(X, Y)
REAL X, Y
    .
    .
    .
READ *, BUSY
IF (BUSY .GT. 10) BUSY = IFIX(X + Y)
    .
    .
    .
BUSY = 2 * BUSY − BUSY ** 2
    .
    .
    .
RETURN
END
```

Note that the name of this integer function is used as a name of an integer variable would be used.

The execution of a RETURN statement returns control to the invoking program unit. Several RETURN's may be contained in a function body; the first encountered during the function execution returns control.

The END statement delimits the function.

▷ FORTRAN 77 does not require a RETURN statement before END; the old standard does. It is a good practice to include it.   ◁

2. HOW TO USE A FUNCTION

A function is used simply by reference to it, i.e., by placing:

$$\text{function name } \underbrace{(\text{list of actual arguments})}_{\text{optional}}$$

essentially anywhere, where a variable may be used to render a value of the same type as this function. The type of a function (like the type of a variable) has to be specified explicitly or implicitly in the program unit that uses the function. To specify the type of the function explicitly, its name alone (without the arguments) has to be listed in an appropriate type statement.

Typically, functions are used in expressions, for example, on the right-hand side of an assignment.

EXAMPLE 8-12

If we have defined a function

```
INTEGER FUNCTION BUSY(X, Y)
```

it may be, for example, referenced (invoked) as follows:

```
   LOAD = 25 * BUSY(A, 27.3)
or WRITE (6, 507) BUSY(C, D)
or IF (BUSY(ARR(10), 1.543) .GT. 1) GOTO 10
```

Note that X and Y are real variables, while the function BUSY itself is of integer type and has to be listed in an INTEGER statement in the program unit that uses this function:

```
   INTEGER BUSY
```

The discussion of argument passing, i.e., the association of actual and dummy arguments, presented in Section B–3 of this chapter, applies to functions as well as subroutines. The essential goal of function use, however, is to obtain a single value that is assigned to the function name.

> The use of functions with output arguments and, in general, the use of functions to pass any values to the invoking program unit other than through the function name lowers the readability of the program, leads to obscure errors, and should be avoided.

To communicate with a function, common blocks may be used along with or instead of arguments (see Section D of this chapter).

The use of functions is illustrated by the following example.

EXAMPLE 8-13

Problem
Cubic roots of a collection of real numbers are to be calculated with precision of 10^{-5}.

Solution
A function CUBRT is designed to calculate the cubic roots with the use of the Newton-Raphson method: successive approximations to the root are computed until the desired precision is reached. The precision is determined as the difference between two successive approximations.

The computation formula for the cubic root of X is

$$R_{n+1} = \frac{1}{3}\left(2R_n + \frac{X}{R_n^2}\right)$$

where

R_{n+1} is the current approximation to the root value
R_n is the previous approximation

For computer computations, the first approximation is taken to be X itself:

$$R_o = X$$

The pseudocode of the function CUBRT follows.

```
* SUCCESSIVE APPROXIMATIONS "NEXT" ARE COMPUTED TO THE
* CUBIC ROOT OF X USING PREVIOUS APPROXIMATION "CUBRT"
Real Function CUBRT(X)
begin
    Real X, NEXT;
*THE ORIGINAL VALUE IS THE FIRST APPROXIMATION
    NEXT ← X;
    repeat
        begin
            CUBRT ←NEXT;
            NEXT ← (2*CUBRT + X/CUBRT**2)/3
        end
    until | CUBRT − NEXT | ≤.000001;
    CUBRT ← NEXT
end
```

The program follows.

```
C     PROGRAM  CUBICS
C     AUTHOR:            DATE:
C
C     CUBIC ROOTS ARE OBTAINED FOR A COLLECTION OF NUMBERS
C
C     ROOTEE - NUMBER WHOSE ROOT IS NEEDED
C
      IMPLICIT REAL (A-Z)
      WRITE (6,501)
  501 FORMAT('     CUBIC ROOT OF', 8X, 'IS')
C
   10 READ (5,502,END = 20) ROOTEE
  502     FORMAT(F12.5)
          WRITE (6,503) ROOTEE, CUBRT(ROOTEE)
  503     FORMAT(3X, F12.5, 3X, F12.5)
      GOTO 10
C
   20 STOP
      END
```

```
C
C     CUBIC ROOTS ARE OBTAINED WITH PRECISION E-5
C           USING NEWTON-RAPHSON METHOD
C
      REAL FUNCTION CUBRT(X)
C
      IMPLICIT REAL (A-Z)
C     THE ORIGINAL VALUE SERVES AS THE FIRST APPROXIMATION
      NEXT = X
 10   CONTINUE
         CUBRT = NEXT
         NEXT = (2. * CUBRT + X / CUBRT ** 2) / 3.
      IF (ABS(CUBRT - NEXT) .GT. .000001) GOTO 10
      CUBRT = NEXT
      RETURN
      END
```

A sample output:

```
        CUBIC ROOT OF         IS
              1.00000      1.00000
            271.25789      6.47333
              3.00000      1.44225
             27.00000      3.00000
```

D. COMMUNICATION THROUGH COMMON BLOCKS

As discussed above in this chapter, independent program units may communicate by passing explicitly listed arguments. The alternative method of communication between program units is through *common blocks:* memory areas, accessible to more than one program unit in a given program. Thus, common blocks hold global data.

To establish such a shared memory area, a COMMON declaration is used. The types of common blocks may be established: *blank common,* a single unnamed area accessible to all program units where it is declared, and *named common,* an area bearing a name and also accessible only to those program units where it is declared. The entire program may have only a single blank common area, but a number of named common blocks, accessible only to the modules with "the need to know."

Common blocks may be used in preference to explicit parameter passing when a number of arguments are shared among several program units. Thus, long argument lists are avoided.

> Common blocks should not be used needlessly instead of explicit argument passing. Their use may lead to errors difficult to locate.

The data in named common blocks may be initialized by a DATA BLOCK subprogram (see Section F of this chapter); it is not possible to initialize data in the blank common block.

1. BLANK COMMON BLOCKS

Ordinarily, blank common blocks are used. The general format of the nonexecutable COMMON statement, when used to establish the blank common block for the given program, is

COMMON list of variable and/or array names (or array declarators)

For example, these two statements together describe the common block in a certain program:

```
REAL X, Y(100, 50), W, Z
COMMON X, Y, W(21), Z
```

As a nonexecutable specification statement, this statement is placed before all the executable statements in the given program unit. For example, COMMON statements may be placed following the type and DIMENSION statements.

An array declarator (i.e., the array name together with the parenthesized dimensions) may be placed either in the type statement, in the DIMENSION statement, or in COMMON, but in not more than one place.

Preferably, place the array declarator in the appropriate type statement, for example,

```
INTEGER ARRAY(100)
COMMON ARRAY
```

or, if the type of the array is implicitly defined by its name, in the COMMON statement, for example,

```
COMMON ITEMS(25)
```

Different names may be used for the items listed in COMMON in various program units. The items are associated by positional correspondence. Thus, the types of items in the same relative position in various program units should be the same.

EXAMPLE 8–14

In the program with the structure shown in Fig. 8–6, the following common block may be declared.

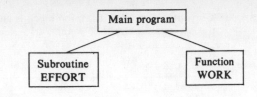

FIGURE 8-6.

main program:	COMMON X, Y, Z(100)
subroutine EFFORT:	COMMON A, B, C(100)
function WORK:	COMMON E, F, G(100)

Thus, the same array is called Z in the main program, C in the subroutine, and G in the function.

A common block constitutes a single area in memory, even though it is accessible to several program units. This method may be used along with explicit argument passing, but a dummy argument may not appear in a COMMON statement.

EXAMPLE 8-15

The following example illustrates simultaneous use of the two means of communication: argument passing and common blocks.

```
C   THIS IS THE MAIN PROGRAM
        INTEGER IND, CLASS(10)
        REAL MARKS(50)
        COMMON CLASS, MARKS, IND
        CALL EVAL(5)
           .
           .
           .
        STOP
        END
C
        SUBROUTINE EVAL(PERF)
        INTEGER PERF, JOB(10), PAR
        REAL GRADES(50)
        COMMON JOB, GRADES, PAR
           .
           .
           .
        RETURN
        END
```

The corresponding layout of the blank common block is shown here.

name used in main program	CLASS	MARKS	IND
	array of 10 integers	array of 50 real numbers	an integer
name used in subroutine EVAL	JOB	GRADES	PAR

The fact that the blank common block is a single memory area has the following implications.

(1) The length of COMMON areas in various program units may differ; the positional correspondence has to be, however, maintained.

This means that only the item(s) appearing last in a COMMON statement may be dropped in certain program units where it is desired.

EXAMPLE 8–16

Consider the program of Example 8–14. It would be legal to have the following declarations:

subroutine EFFORT: COMMON A, B
function WORK: COMMON E

Naturally, if such communication were wanted, it should be accomplished through explicit argument passing.

It would be illegal to have, for example, in subroutine EFFORT:

COMMON A, C(100)

If conforming to the rule of positional correspondence creates problems, "artificial" variables/arrays of appropriate type may be provided in a COMMON declaration to "fill the gaps."

(2) Restructuring of arrays in the common block is possible but should be treated with utmost care. For example, what is a two-dimensional array in one program unit may be considered a linear array in another, once the FORTRAN memory allocation scheme for arrays is considered (see Chapter 6–A–4).

EXAMPLE 8–17

If all variables and arrays are of the same type, the following are legal declarations in a certain program:

Main program: COMMON K(3), L, M(2)
Subroutine: COMMON NT, N(2, 2)

This memory layout results:

name used in
main program

K(1)	K(2)	K(3)	L	M(1)	M(2)

name used in   NT   N(1, 1) N(2, 1) N(1, 2) N(2, 2)   not accessible
subroutine   to subroutine

Note how error-prone is such usage.

(3) Entities in a blank common block may not be initialized by a DATA statement (or a BLOCK DATA subprogram).

(4) A blank common block exists throughout program execution. Once a program unit with an access to blank common stores a value there, any other unit with an access will find it there (unless it has been modified in the meantime).

(5) Several blank COMMON declarations may be provided in a program unit; their effect is equivalent to having a single aggregate one.

EXAMPLE 8–18

When placed in the same program unit, these two declarations:

```
COMMON WIDTH(10)
COMMON LENGTH
```

are equivalent to

```
COMMON WIDTH(10), LENGTH
```

2. NAMED COMMON BLOCKS

A program may contain only a single blank common block that is shared by all program units with the corresponding COMMON declaration. If it is desired to have certain other data blocks shared by some, but not all, program units, *named common* blocks are established (they are also called *labeled common*).

The general form of the COMMON statement, when used to establish named common blocks, is

```
COMMON/block name/common block list . . . /block name/common block list
```

where a common block list consists of variable and/or array names (or array declarators), separated by commas.

Each list enumerates the items located in the block whose name is enclosed in slashes.

> For readability, insert a couple of blanks before every "opening" slash.

For example,

```
COMMON /DESCR/LENGTH(5), WEIGHT /AGE/CLASS(10)
```

The rules of the use of the COMMON statement presented for the blank common in the preceding section apply.

The named common facility restricts access to parts of the overall common area to only those programs that need to use the data contained therein.

The same name of the common block has to be used in all program units that are sharing it, while the names used to refer to the variables and arrays located in the block may differ among these program units.

Along with the access to a named common block (or several such blocks), a program unit may have access to the blank common area of the program. A single COMMON statement may be used to establish access to both. In such a statement, if the blank common is listed first, its name is simply omitted; otherwise, the blank common is provided with a "blank name" of //. For example, the statements

```
COMMON ABC(10), LOC /DUES/X(5) /MEMB/A, B
```
and
```
COMMON /DUES/X(5) //ABC(10), LOC /MEMB/A, B
```

declare the same common blocks, the blank common containing ABC(10), LOC.

Since a single blank common exists for the program, it may be declared only once in the given program unit.

EXAMPLE 8–19

We have a program with the structure shown in Fig. 8–7.

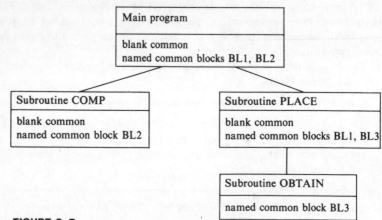

FIGURE 8–7.

In fulfillment of this structure the following COMMON statements will be contained in the program units:

Main program: COMMON A, B(10) /BL1/C(25) /BL2/D(50), E
Subroutine COMP: COMMON V, W(10) /BL2/X(50), Y
Subroutine PLACE: COMMON Z /BL1/R(25) /BL3/P(15, 15)
Subroutine OBTAIN: COMMON /BL3/S(15, 15)

Implicit variable and array types are assumed.

Each program unit may access only the common blocks declared in it. The access map is shown in Table 8–2.

TABLE 8–2. Access map to common blocks and names used for the variables and arrays located in them

program unit	BLANK COMMON	NAMED COMMON BLOCKS		
		BL1	BL2	BL3
Main program	A, B(10)	C(25)	D(50), E	no access
Subroutine COMP	V, W(10)	no access	X(50), Y	no access
Subroutine PLACE	Z	R(25)	no access	P(15, 15)
Subroutine OBTAIN	no access	no access	no access	S(15, 15)

The following rules apply to every named common block.

(1) The rule of positional correspondence within each block applies as in the blank common.
(2) The length of every named common block bearing the same name must be the same in every program unit (note that this distinguishes the named common from the blank common).
(3) The values of the entities in a named common block may be initialized with a BLOCK DATA subprogram (see Section F). This cannot be done for a blank common block.
(4) A named common block exists only throughout the execution of the program unit where it is declared.

If it happens to be declared in the main program (as BL1 or BL2 in Example 8–19), it exists throughout the execution of the entire program and thus behaves in this respect like a blank common (see the section above). If, however, it is declared in a subprogram, it is established when the first subprogram with such a declaration is entered and destroyed when the return from this subprogram occurs. It exists, however, in all the subprograms invoked by the given one, where it is declared. For example, block BL3 in Example 8–19 exists only during the execution of the subroutine PLACE (which includes the execution of the subroutine OBTAIN). Had it been also declared in the subroutine COMP, no values could have been transmitted in it to the subroutine PLACE, since it would have been destroyed after the return from either of these subroutines to the main program.

▷ In FORTRAN 77, the contents of a named common block area may be preserved with a SAVE statement (such discussion is beyond our scope here) ◁

E. EXAMPLE WITH APPLICATION OF BINARY SEARCH

This section presents an example of the design and documentation of a larger modular program.

EXAMPLE 8–20

Problem

A program for periodical maintenance of a payroll file is to be produced.

The maintenance program is not to produce payroll; its task is to update the payroll file by introducing into it the changes that have taken place during the week, so that the payroll may be produced subsequently. Relatively few such changes are to be expected.

A simple program is desired, even at a cost of certain execution time inefficiencies. To provide for future extensions to the system, a highly modular system is to be designed.

System Analysis

The payroll file will consist of employee records, placed one to a card. Each record will contain the following fields (data items):

SOCSEC—employee Social Security number
RATE—hourly wage rate
HOURS—number of hours worked
DEDUCT—number of tax deductions

The file is ordered (sorted) in the ascending order of SOCSEC. This field, which uniquely identifies a record, is the key of the file.

Records of the payroll file, called further master records, will have the make-up shown:

name of field	SOCSEC	RATE	HOURS	DEDUCT
FORMAT descriptor	I10	F10.2	F10.2	I10

Note the selection of a uniform field width of 10: this simplifies manual processing of cards.

The changes to be made during the updating of a master file are collected in the transaction file, whose records are accumulated between the update runs. There are three kinds of transaction records: Modify ("hourly rate went up" or "employee worked 4 hours fewer than usual"), Delete ("employee was separated"), and Insert ("new employee was hired").

A transaction file also contains a single record per card. The nature of the transaction is distinguished by the ID field of the record. The transaction file, composed of transaction records, is not sorted.

Transaction records have the make-up shown.

(a) Modify:

name	KEY	ID	TRRATE	TRHRS	TRDED	FIELD
		1				1/2/3
descriptor	I10	I10	F10.2	F10.2	I10	I10

(b) Delete:

name	KEY	ID
		2
descriptor	I10	I10

(c) Insert:

name	KEY	ID	TRRATE	TRHRS	TRDED
		3			
descriptor	I10	I10	F10.2	F10.2	I10

In the case of the Modify transaction, the field to be modified is identified by FIELD (e.g., if FIELD = 2, the new value of HOURS is given). Thus, if two fields of a master record are to be modified (deemed to be rare), two transaction records are presented. The SOCSEC cannot be modified.

The other transaction record fields correspond to the master record fields as follows:

$$KEY \longleftrightarrow SOCSEC \qquad TRHRS \longleftrightarrow HOURS$$
$$TRRATE \longleftrightarrow RATE \qquad TRDED \longleftrightarrow DEDUCT$$

ALGORITHM. INITIAL FORM

Due to the small number of transaction records and the desire to keep the program simple, the transaction file will not be sorted. This calls for the following algorithm.

*Maintenance of sorted master file
begin
    Input master file;
    Process all transactions against master file;
    Output new master file
end

ALGORITHM. FIRST REFINEMENT

*Maintenance of sorted master file
begin
    Input master file;
*Process all transactions against master file
    while there are more transactions **do**
        begin
            Input next transaction;
            Search for the master record with the key
                specified by the transaction;
            if transaction is Modify **then**
              Modify master record
            else
              if transaction is Delete **then**
                Delete master record
              else
                *transaction is Insert *
                Insert new master record
        end;
    Output new master file
end

At this point the need for five modules has been identified: The main program (to read in transactions), and Search, Delete, Insert, and Modify modules. The dependence among these is shown in the structure chart (see Fig. 8–9, where the Search module is called BINSRC as the result of further analysis).

We conclude that a search algorithm is needed to find the position in the file of a master record identified by its key. Since the master file is sorted, binary search may be employed, as explained below.

BINARY SEARCH

The purpose of a search is to locate in a file a record identified by its key.

If there is no dependence between the position of a record in the file and the value of its key, then there is no alternative to a *sequential search:* starting with the first record, the keys of the records in the file are compared with the given key until the needed record is found (or until the end of the file is reached without the record having been found).

Sequential search is inherently slow: a successful search requires on the average $N/2$ comparisons in a file holding N records.

Much faster is the binary search, applicable exclusively to files sorted on the key used in the search. *Binary search* resembles a procedure we would use to look up a word in an unfamiliar dictionary. Let us assume the file is sorted in ascending order. First, the middle of the file is checked: if our look-up key is smaller than that in the middle of the file, the search has to continue in the first half of the file; if our key is larger than the middle one, the search will be confined to the second half of the file. We then search the selected half in the same way by checking its middle record, etc. The search is completed when our key equals the one of the file record.

Binary search requires, on the average, about $\log_2 N$ comparisons to find a record in a file of N records; it is thus much faster than sequential search.

The following is the pseudocode of the search routine.

```
*Binary search:
*A file consisting of N records,
*with the keys KEY(I), is searched for the key GIVEN.
*The value of INDEX is the position of the record with this
*key in the file; if INDEX = 0, the file does not contain such a record.
```

```
Subroutine BINARY(KEY, N, GIVEN, INDEX)
begin
      Integer N, KEY(I), GIVEN, INDEX, LOW, HIGH;
      LOW ← 1; * the lowest position in the subfile being searched *
      HIGH ← N; * the highest position in the subfile being searched *
* The position INDEX of the record with the key GIVEN in
* the file is determined
SRC: while LOW ≤ HIGH do
            begin
                  INDEX ← (LOW + HIGH) ÷ 2; * integer division*
                  if GIVEN < KEY(INDEX) then
                        HIGH ← INDEX − 1 * look in the first half*
                  else
                        if GIVEN > KEY(INDEX) then
                           LOW ← INDEX + 1 *look in the second half*
                        else
                           exit SRC      *found*
* value of INDEX is returned
            end;
      if LOW > HIGH then *not found*
         INDEX ← 0
      else
end
```

Note that **exit** statement causes the transfer of control past the construct bearing the label indicated, that means, in our case, past the entire **while-do** construct.

The use of this subroutine is illustrated, with the following list of steps during binary search for N = 9, GIVEN = 300.

BEFORE FIRST COMPARISON	BEFORE SECOND COMPARISON	BEFORE THIRD COMPARISON
←—LOW		
5	5	5
21	21	21
73	73	73
124	124	124
INDEX→ 241	241	241
300	300	→300
450	→450	450
701	701	701
715 ←—HIGH	715	715

$$\text{LOW} = 1$$
$$\text{HIGH} = 9$$
$$\text{INDEX} = \left\lfloor\frac{1+9}{2}\right\rfloor = 5$$

integer part of

$$\text{LOW} = 6$$
$$\text{HIGH} = 9$$
$$\text{INDEX} = \left\lfloor\frac{6+9}{2}\right\rfloor = 7$$

$$\text{LOW} = 6$$
$$\text{HIGH} = 6$$
$$\text{INDEX} = \left\lfloor\frac{6+6}{2}\right\rfloor = 6$$

This subroutine will be adapted for use in our payroll system.

ALGORITHM. FINAL REFINEMENT

The interfaces between the modules (i.e., arguments and global blocks) are more precisely specified in the interface table to follow. Common blocks are denoted with **Global** statements.

```
* Maintenance of sorted master file for payroll application
begin
      Integer N, GIVEN, INDEX;
      Global MASTER(I); * records of master file *
* Input master file
      N← 0; * N − number of records in master file*
      while there are more master records do
            begin
                  Input next master record;
                  N← N + 1
            end;
* Process all transactions against master file
      while there are more transactions do
            begin
                  Input next transaction (its key is GIVEN);
* Find the position (INDEX) of the master record with key GIVEN;
* if no such record exists, INDEX is the position of the
* immediate preceding record
                  Call BINSRC(N, GIVEN, INDEX);
                  if transaction is Modify then
                        Call MODIFY(INDEX, transaction record)
```

```
                    else
                        if transaction is Delete then
                            begin
                                    Call DELETE(INDEX, N); N ← N − 1
                            end
                            else * transaction is Insert *
                                begin
                                        Call INSERT(INDEX, new record, N); N ←N + 1
                                end
            end;
* Output new master file
        while N > 0 do
            begin
                    Output next master record; N ← N − 1
            end
end
* The position (INDEX) of the record with the key GIVEN in
* the file MASTER with key SOCSEC is determined.
* If the record is not found, INDEX is the position of the
* record with the immediate smaller key.
Subroutine BINSRC(N, GIVEN, INDEX)
begin
        Integer N, GIVEN, INDEX;
        Global MASTER(I); *every record contains a field SOCSEC(I) *
        LOW ← 1;
        HIGH ← N;
SRC: while LOW ≤ HIGH do
            begin
                    INDEX ← (LOW + HIGH) ÷ 2;
                    if GIVEN < SOCSEC(INDEX) then
                            HIGH ← INDEX − 1
                    else
                            if GIVEN > SOCSEC(INDEX) then
                                    LOW ← INDEX + 1
                            else
                                    exit SRC
            end;
* If search is unsuccessful, INDEX is to be the position of
* the record with the immediate smaller key
        if LOW > HIGH then
            INDEX ← HIGH * check that this is so! *
        else
end
* A master record is modified
Subroutine MODIFY(INDEX, transaction record)
begin
        Integer INDEX;
```

Global MASTER(I);
appropriate field of MASTER(INDEX) ← new value from
transaction record
end
* A master record is deleted
Subroutine DELETE(INDEX, N)
begin
    Integer INDEX, N;
    Global MASTER(I);
* Move down the records following the position INDEX
    I ← INDEX;
    while I < N **do**
        begin
            MASTER(I) ← MASTER(I + 1); I ← I + 1
        end
end
* A master record is inserted following the record in the position INDEX
Subroutine INSERT(INDEX, new record, N)
begin
    Integer INDEX;
    Global MASTER(I);
* Make space for new record by moving up the records that
* will follow it
    I ← N;
    while I ≥ INDEX + 1 **do**
        begin
            MASTER(I + 1) ← MASTER(I); I ← I − 1
        end;
* Place the new record
    MASTER(INDEX + 1) ← new record
end

Note that the subroutines DELETE and INSERT call for a large amount of data movement. This is warranted if few transactions are to be processed and a simple system is desired.

In a more elaborate system, the transaction file would be sorted before the updating run. Instead of reading in the master file fully before the run, it would have been read in incrementally as needed to process the transactions. Simultaneously, the new master would be created on the output device.

REPRESENTATION OF RECORDS IN FORTRAN

Records (nodes), i.e., data structures consisting of fields with their own names, are represented in FORTRAN as a set of arrays, with each array representing a single field.

Thus, the representation of our master file in FORTRAN is as shown in Fig. 8-8.

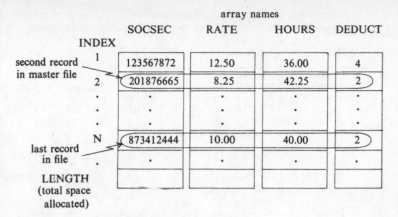

FIGURE 8-8. A record representation in FORTRAN

As can be seen from Fig. 8-8, a single record consists of the ordered set of array elements with the same subscript values in their respective arrays.

STRUCTURE CHART AND INTERFACE TABLE

Our program (such larger programs are often called systems) is further described by its structure chart, which shows the dependence between the modules (program units) and the interface table that specifies the data items passed as arguments and stored in global (common) areas.

A structure chart of the program is shown in Figure 8-9.

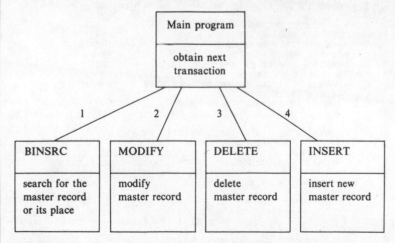

FIGURE 8-9. Structure chart

The interface table (Table 8–3) refers to the interfaces as numbered in the structure chart. The names of the actual arguments are given.

TABLE 8–3. Interface table

INTERFACE NUMBER	INPUT ARGUMENTS	OUTPUT ARGUMENTS	ACCESS TO COMMON BLOCKS
1	KEY, N	INDEX, FOUND	/IDENT/, /ATTRIB/
2	INDEX, TRRATE, TRHRS, TRDED, FIELD		/ATTRIB/
3	INDEX, N		/IDENT/, /ATTRIB/
4	INDEX, N, KEY, TRRATE, TRHRS, TRDED		/IDENT/, /ATTRIB/

Common blocks: /IDENT/SOCSEC
/ATTRIB/RATE, HOURS, DEDUCT

FORTRAN PROGRAM

The following is the FORTRAN implementation of the payroll maintenance program. The program is documented by its own text, the pseudocode, the structure chart, and the interface table.

Note that certain error-checking facilities have been included.

```
C    PROGRAM: PAYROLL
C    AUTHOR:              DATE:
C
C    PAYROLL FILE LOCATED ON CARDS IS MAINTAINED
C
C    N - NUMBER OF MASTER RECORDS
C    SOCSEC - SOCIAL SECURITY NUMBER       - KEY
C    RATE - HOURLY WAGE RATE               - TRRATE
C    HOURS - HOURS WORKED                  - TRHRS
C    DEDUCT - NUMBER OF TAX DEDUCTIONS     - TRDED
C    ID - TRANSACTION ID
C    INDEX - POSITION OF RECORD AFFECTED BY TRANSACTION
C    FIELD - TO BE MODIFIED
C    FOUND - IS THE RECORD IN FILE?
C
C
         INTEGER KEY, ID, TRDED, FIELD, INDEX, N,
     +           SOCSEC(500), DEDUCT(500)
         REAL TRRATE, TRHRS, RATE(500), HOURS(500)
         COMMON /IDENT/SOCSEC   /ATTRIB/RATE, HOURS, DEDUCT
C
C    INPUT MASTER FILE
         N = 0
     10 CONTINUE
             N = N + 1
             READ (5,501) SOCSEC(N), RATE(N), HOURS(N), DEDUCT(N)
    501      FORMAT(I10, 2F10.2, I10)
         IF (SOCSEC(N) .NE. 0) GOTO 10
         N = N - 1
```

```
C
C     OBTAIN AND PROCESS NEXT TRANSACTION
C
   20 CONTINUE
             READ (5,502,END=70) KEY, ID, TRRATE, TRHRS, TRDED,
      +                FIELD
  502        FORMAT(2I10, 2F10.2, 2I10)
             WRITE (6,502) KEY, ID, TRRATE, TRHRS, TRDED,
      +                FIELD
C
C     FIND THE CORRESPONDING MASTER RECORD
C
             CALL BINSRC(KEY, N, INDEX, FOUND)
C
             GOTO (30,40,50), ID
C
C     NO SUCH TRANSACTION
             PRINT *, 'ERRONEOUS TRANSACTION CODE', KEY
             GOTO 60
C
C     RECORD IS TO BE MODIFIED
   30        CONTINUE
             IF (.NOT. FOUND) THEN
                 PRINT *, 'ATTEMPT TO MODIFY NONEXISTENT',
      +                 ' RECORD', KEY
                 GOTO 60
             ENDIF
             CALL MODIFY(INDEX, TRRATE, TRHRS, TRDED, FIELD)
             GOTO 60
C
C     RECORD IS TO BE DELETED
   40        CONTINUE
             IF (.NOT. FOUND) THEN
                 PRINT *, 'ATTEMPT TO DELETE NONEXISTENT',
      +                 ' RECORD', KEY
                 GOTO 60
             ENDIF
             CALL DELETE(INDEX, N)
             N = N - 1
             GOTO 60
C
C     RECORD IS TO BE INSERTED
   50        CONTINUE
             IF (FOUND) THEN
                 PRINT *, 'ATTEMPT TO INSERT RECORD WITH',
                         ' DUPLICATE KEY', KEY
                 GOTO 60
             ENDIF
             CALL INSERT(INDEX, N, KEY, TRRATE,
      +                 TRHRS, TRDED)
             N = N + 1
   60        CONTINUE
      GOTO 20
   70 CONTINUE
C
C     OUTPUT NEW MASTER FILE
C     (IT IS ASSUMED THAT '2' IS THE DEVICE CODE
C     OF THE CARD PUNCH)
      WRITE (2,501) (SOCSEC(I), RATE(I), HOURS(I),
      +              DEDUCT(I), I=1,N)
      STOP
      END
```

```
C
C     POSITION (INDEX) OF RECORD WITH THE KEY 'GIVEN'
C     IS DETERMINED;  IF SUCH RECORD IS NOT FOUND, INDEX
C     IS THE POSITION OF THE PRECEDING RECORD
C
      SUBROUTINE BINSRC(GIVEN, N, INDEX, FOUND)
C
C     BINARY SEARCH TECHNIQUE IS USED
C          INPUT ARGUMENTS:
C     GIVEN - KEY SEARCHED FOR
C     N - NUMBER OF RECORDS IN FILE
C          OUTPUT ARGUMENTS:
C     INDEX - OF THE GIVEN (IF FOUND) OR PRECEDING RECORD
C     FOUND - HAS THE RECORD BEEN FOUND?
C          OTHER VARIABLES:
C     SOCSEC(I) - FILE KEY
C     LOW, HIGH - THE LOWEST AND THE HIGHEST INDEX CONSIDERED
C
      IMPLICIT INTEGER (A-Z)
      LOGICAL FOUND
      COMMON /IDENT/SOCSEC(500)
C
      LOW = 1
      HIGH = N
C     BY HALVING THE SUBFILE SEARCHED, LOOK FOR THE 'GIVEN'
   10 IF (LOW .GT. HIGH) GOTO 20
          INDEX = (LOW + HIGH)/2
          IF (GIVEN .LT. SOCSEC(INDEX)) HIGH = INDEX - 1
          IF (GIVEN .GT. SOCSEC(INDEX)) LOW = INDEX + 1
          IF (GIVEN .EQ. SOCSEC(INDEX)) GOTO 20
          GOTO 10
   20 CONTINUE
C
C     DETERMINE WHETHER SEARCH WAS SUCCESSFUL; IF NOT,
C          OBTAIN POSITION OF THE PRECEDING RECORD
      IF (LOW .LE. HIGH) THEN
          FOUND = .TRUE.
      ELSE
          FOUND = .FALSE.
          INDEX = HIGH
      ENDIF
      RETURN
      END
C
C     MODIFY A RECORD
C
      SUBROUTINE MODIFY(INDEX, NEWRAT, NEWHRS, NEWDED, FIELD)
C
C               INPUT ARGUMENTS:
C     INDEX - OF THE RECORD TO BE MODIFIED
C     FIELD - TO BE MODIFIED
C     NEWRAT, NEWHRS, NEWDED - NEW VALUES OF DATA ITEMS
C
      INTEGER INDEX, FIELD, NEWDED
      REAL NEWRAT, NEWHRS, RATE(500), HOURS(500), DEDUCT(500)
      COMMON /ATTRIB/RATE, HOURS, DEDUCT
C
      GOTO (10,20,30), FIELD
   10     RATE(INDEX) = NEWRAT
          RETURN
```

```
      20 CONTINUE
             HOURS(INDEX) = NEWHRS
             RETURN
      30 CONTINUE
             DEDUCT(INDEX) = NEWDED
         RETURN
         END
C
C  DELETE A RECORD
C
         SUBROUTINE DELETE(INDEX, N)
C
C             INPUT ARGUMENTS:
C  INDEX - OF RECORD TO BE DELETED
C  N - NUMBER OF RECORDS IN FILE
C
         INTEGER INDEX, N, SOCSEC(500), DEDUCT(500)
         REAL RATE(500), HOURS(500)
         COMMON /IDENT/SOCSEC  /ATTRIB/RATE, HOURS, DEDUCT
C
C  MOVE RECORDS DOWN
         DO 10 I = INDEX, N - 1
             SOCSEC(I) = SOCSEC(I+1)
             RATE(I) = RATE(I+1)
             HOURS(I) = HOURS(I+1)
             DEDUCT(I) = DEDUCT(I+1)
      10 CONTINUE
         RETURN
         END
C
C  INSERT A RECORD
C
         SUBROUTINE INSERT(INDEX, N, NEWSS, NEWRAT, NEWHRS, NEWDED)
C
C             INPUT ARGUMENTS:
C  INDEX - OF THE RECORD PRECEDING THE ONE TO BE INSERTED
C  N - NUMBER OF RECORDS IN FILE
C  NEWSS, NEWRAT, NEWHRS, NEWDED - FIELDS OF NEW RECORD
C
         INTEGER INDEX, N, NEWSS, NEWDED, SOCSEC(500),DEDUCT(500)
         REAL NEWRAT, NEWHRS, RATE(500), HOURS(500)
         COMMON /IDENT/SOCSEC  /ATTRIB/RATE, HOURS, DEDUCT
C
C  MOVE RECORDS TO FOLLOW THE NEW ONE UP
         DO 10 I = N, INDEX+1, -1
             SOCSEC(I+1) = SOCSEC(I)
             RATE(I+1) = RATE(I)
             HOURS(I+1) = HOURS(I)
             DEDUCT(I+1) = DEDUCT(I)
      10 CONTINUE
C
C  INSERT NEW RECORD
         SOCSEC(INDEX+1) = NEWSS
         RATE(INDEX+1) = NEWRAT
         HOURS(INDEX+1) = NEWHRS
         DEDUCT(INDEX+1) = NEWDED
         RETURN
         END
```

When these transactions were processed:

```
187610002        1      13.00        0.00             0        1
334566780        2       0.00        0.00             0        0
403400000        3       8.50       40.00             2        0
800000000        2       0.00        0.00             0        0
```

against   ⎰ 135467452   12.50   36.00   2
this

```
against  ┌ 135467452     12.50       36.00             2
this     │ 187610002      9.50       45.25             4
old master 334566780     10.00       36.00             3
file,    │ 404890324     10.00       40.00             1
         └ 412389730     10.50       42.50             5
this error      0         0.00        0.00             0
message  ──→ ATTEMPT TO DELETE NONEXISTENT RECORD 800000000
and this  ┌ 135467452    12.50       36.00             2
new master│ 187610002    13.00       45.25             4
file     ⟨ 403400000      8.50       40.00             2
         │ 404890324     10.00       40.00             1
         └ 412389730     10.50       42.50             5
```

were generated.

F. BLOCK DATA SUBPROGRAMS

To initialize variables and arrays in a named common block, a separate program unit, called BLOCK DATA, has to be used. (Data in blank common blocks cannot be initialized.) This subprogram has the following general form:

BLOCK DATA
nonexecutable statements such as: type statements
                                      DIMENSION
                                      COMMON
                                      EQUIVALENCE
DATA statement(s)
END

Note the absence of RETURN statement.

▷ FORTRAN 77 permits the naming of this subprogram, e.g., BLOCK DATA VALUES, and thus the use of several such subprograms with different names in a single program (but no more than one without a name). ◁

This subprogram, consisting entirely of nonexecutable statements, is processed independently during the program translation.

One BLOCK DATA statement may serve to initialize data in several named common blocks. A named common block has to be specified fully in a BLOCK DATA subprogram, even when this subprogram is used to initialize only some of its entities.

A BLOCK DATA subprogram always includes a DATA statement that actually initializes the data (see Chapter 6–B). Other statements in the subprogram are the specification statements needed to describe the type of the entities and to declare the dimensions of the arrays.

EXAMPLE 8–21

This subroutine uses the named common block PERF:

```
SUBROUTINE WORK(X, Y)
REAL GRADES(20), VALUE, X, Y
COMMON/PERF/GRADES(20), VALUE, Z
      .
      .
      .
RETURN
END
```

This BLOCK DATA subprogram, enclosed with the subroutine WORK, initializes GRADES and Z:

```
BLOCK DATA
REAL GRADES(20), VALUE, Z
COMMON /PERF/GRADES(20), VALUE, Z
DATA GRADES/20*1./, Z/17./
END
```

G. MULTIPLE ENTRY AND RETURN POINTS (FORTRAN 77)

Multiple entry points in a subprogram and multiple return points in a calling program are features available only in the new standard, FORTRAN 77.

1. MULTIPLE ENTRIES TO A SUBPROGRAM

A subprogram (function or subroutine) is usually executed beginning with the first executable statement in its text. However, ENTRY statement(s) may be placed in the subprogram to provide one or more alternative entry points. The ENTRY statement has the following general form:

ENTRY entry point name <u>(list of dummy arguments)</u>

when present

For example,

```
ENTRY HERE(X1, X2)
```

The execution of the subprogram begins with the ENTRY statement named in the invocation and proceeds until a RETURN or the END statement is reached.

The list of dummy arguments of an ENTRY statement may be wholly different from the list stated in the SUBROUTINE or the FUNCTION statement of the subprogram. This list has to agree, however, with the list of actual arguments in the invocation (call).

If an ENTRY statement is placed in a subrotine, it is treated like a SUB-ROUTINE statement (see Section B–1 of this chapter); in an external function it is treated like a FUNCTION statement (see Section C–1 of this chapter).

Every ENTRY statement defines, as it were, a separate subprogram as a part of the body of another subprogram.

EXAMPLE 8–22

A correspondence between entry points and calls for two program units is shown in Fig. 8–10.

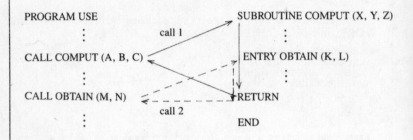

FIGURE 8–10.

An ENTRY statement may not be placed within a DO loop or an IF-THEN-(ELSEIF)-ENDIF construct.

2. MULTIPLE RETURNS TO A CALLING PROGRAM UNIT

When a RETURN statement in a subroutine is executed, control passes to the statement following the CALL. In FORTRAN 77, alternate return points from a subroutine (never a function) may be specified as follows:

(1) In the CALL statement, the return points are listed as labels of statements in the calling program, each label preceded by an asterisk, for example,

    CALL WORK(X, Y, ∗100, ∗240)

These labels indicate first, second, etc., return points.

(2) In the subroutine
   (a) the SUBROUTINE statement contains asterisks in positions corresponding to the alternate return points listed in the actual argument list; for example,

        SUBROUTINE WORK(A, B, ∗, ∗)

(b) the RETURN statements are numbered, with the number indicating the desired return point; for example,

RETURN 2

If this statement is encountered during the execution of our subroutine
WORK, control will return to the statement with label 240 in the calling
program.

EXAMPLE 8-23

In these two program units, the execution of the RETURN statements
shown would cause the transfer of control to the indicated statements in
the calling program.

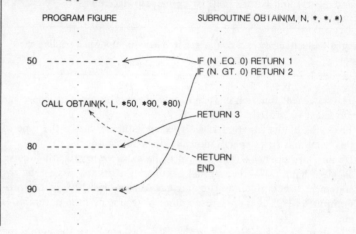

H. STATEMENT FUNCTIONS

If a certain expression is to be used several times in a given program unit,
albeit with different variables and/or array elements, a *statement function*
consisting of a single assignment statement may be defined to compute its
value.

Since a statement function is used to compute a value of a single expression, it resembles an assignment statement. The statement that defines the
statement function is placed within the program unit where the function is
to be used; the function is undefined in other program units.

The use of a statement function is similar to that of an external or an intrinsic function; i.e., a function is invoked simply by reference to it.

The usefulness of this feature is quite limited.

1. HOW TO DEFINE A STATEMENT FUNCTION

A statement function is defined by a single statement of the following form:

statement function name (list of dummy arguments) = expression

optional

For example,

VARIAN(AV, VAL) = (X − AV) ** 2 / VAL

The following explains the definition of a statement function.

(1) The statement is to be placed after all nonexecutable specification statements in the program unit (i.e., after type, DIMENSION, etc., statements) and before the first executable statement.

> Surround this statement with comments; it is easy to miss when reading the program.

(2) The statement function is defined only in the program unit where the statement is located.
(3) The value of the function is assigned to its name; hence the type of this name has to be specified explicitly or implicitly.
(4) Dummy arguments ought always to be variable names; they serve as place-holders for the actual arguments that are passed to the statement function. Thus they are not known elsewhere in the program unit. Even if there are no dummy arguments, the parentheses stay: ( ).
(5) The expression is evaluated in the usual fashion, with the actual arguments substituted for the dummy ones.

▷ FORTRAN IV disallows the use of array elements in the expression; this limitation has been dropped in FORTRAN 77. ◁

All other values needed to evaluate the expression are obtained at the point of reference. For example, when the function VARIAN above is used, the values of AV and VAL will be passed as arguments, but the value of variable X will be obtained as usual.

2. HOW TO USE A STATEMENT FUNCTION

A statement function is used, like any other function, by placing

statement function name (list of actual arguments)

optional

essentially anywhere where a variable of the same type may be used to obtain a value.

When such use is made, the actual arguments (which may be, for example, expressions) are evaluated if needed and substituted for the dummy arguments in corresponding positions. Then the function is evaluated at the point of reference, and the obtained value is substituted for it. Thus, the usual correspondence between the actual and the dummy argument list in type and number of arguments should be maintained.

EXAMPLE 8–24

A program unit may include the following statements:

```
        REAL A, B, C, V, W, X, Y, Z
C   FUNCTION DISCR COMPUTES THE DISCRIMINANT OF A QUADRATIC
C   EQUATION
        DISCR(A, B, C) = B ** 2 − 4. * A * C
C
        .
        .
        .
        IF (DISCR(X, Y, Z) .LT. 0) GOTO 10
        .
        .
        .
        V = 2. + SQRT(DISCR(2., V, W))
        .
        .
        .
```

9

PROCESSING OF CHARACTER STRINGS AND LOGICAL DATA

FORTRAN was initially developed to express algorithms for numerical data processing. Thus, its facilities for the manipulation of character strings or, in other words, text, were originally rudimentary.

FORTRAN IV and other systems conforming to the previous standard do not provide explicit facilities for string processing. It is, however, possible to manipulate character strings by storing them in arrays of other data types, usually in integer arrays.

With the passage of time, computers have been increasingly called upon to process symbolic information such as printed text. The need has arisen to expand FORTRAN in this direction.

FORTRAN 77, the new standard, provides character data as a distinct data type, together with facilities for their manipulation. In this, the new standard follows the WATFIV modification of old FORTRAN; this is also the most significant expansion of the language by the new standard.

In the present chapter, both character processing in systems resembling FORTRAN IV and that in FORTRAN 77 systems are discussed. While for the sake of program portability the new standard allows for text processing using the indirect techniques presented in Section A, programs written in FORTRAN 77 ought to employ explicit CHARACTER type data, which practice promotes clarity and succinctness.

Logical data may be manipulated in FORTRAN as a distinct data type. This type of data, with only two possible values—.TRUE. and .FALSE.—leads to simpler algorithms and processing efficiencies in certain applications.

A. PROCESSING OF CHARACTER STRINGS AS DATA OF OTHER TYPES (FORTRAN IV)

In the FORTRAN implementations that follow the old (1966) standard, and thus in FORTRAN IV, there is no provision for explicit processing of text through the use of a distinct data type.

Thus, characters are stored as so-called *Hollerith constants* in locations corresponding to integer, real, or logical variables and arrays. It is most convenient, and thus generally practiced, to store character strings in integer variables and arrays. Usual arithmetic operations are, of course, meaningless in the case of such entities. To manipulate these entities, we may assign the value of one character-valued entity to another one, or use a comparison in a logical IF statement.

1. PRINTING OF FIXED TEXT

To print a fixed text, it is included in a FORMAT statement with an H edit descriptor, as discussed in Chapter 5–I; for example,

```
    WRITE (6,514)
514 FORMAT(10X, 11HTEMPERATURE)
```

The string of the form

$$n\underbrace{Hhh \ldots h}_{n \text{ characters}}$$

is known as a *Hollerith constant*.

Most pre-FORTRAN-77 compilers allow Hollerith constants to be presented instead in single quotes, e.g.,

```
514 FORMAT(10X, 'TEMPERATURE')
```

This option should be used if available.

2. HOW TO HANDLE VARIABLE CHARACTER DATA

Since FORTRAN IV does not provide character data as a distinct data type, character strings have to be stored in variables and arrays of integer, real, or logical type. Usually, integer variables and arrays are employed for this purpose. Thus, a variable or an array of integer type is assigned Hollerith (i.e., character) data. This may occur as the result of:

(1) initialization with a DATA statement, for example,

```
    DATA NAME/4HJOHN/
```

(2) input/output with the use of an A edit descriptor (see Section 4 below);

(3) assignment of the value of another integer variable holding character data (note that assignment of a numerical value to a variable holding characters does not make sense);

(4) passing of a Hollerith constant as an actual argument through a call to a subroutine whose corresponding dummy argument is of the integer type.

It is the programmer's responsibility to remember which entities hold character data and to manipulate them accordingly.

3. HOW CHARACTERS ARE STORED IN MEMORY

Characters are represented in computer memory with the use of character codes. Expressed in such a code, a single character occupies seven or eight bits of storage (for example, in one of the two most popular codes, the character "A" reads 11000001).

The number of bits in a single memory location depends on the computer model. Very frequently this number is 16 (in the case of most minicomputers) or 32 (in the case of many large machines, such as IBM 360-370 mainframes).

If we assume an eight-bit character code, a single location may thus store up to two or four characters (in general, one to ten characters are stored in a location by various computer models). Whenever the number of characters stored in such a location is smaller than this maximum, the characters are placed on the left, and the rest of the location is filled with the code image of a blank (space), which is one of the characters, of course.

A memory location may be given a name in the program and thus become a variable or an array element. Its contents may be accordingly obtained or modified. As discussed in the previous section, to store character data we usually set up integer variables and arrays. If the string to be stored fits into a single location, a variable may be used to hold it; longer strings are stored in one-dimensional arrays (see next section).

EXAMPLE 9–1

Assuming that our computer stores four characters per location and that the value of the variable NAME is JOHN, we have:

NAME

J	O	H	N

where the entire box represents symbolically the contents of a single memory location.

If the value of the array element NAMES(5) is JOE, we have

NAMES (5)

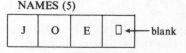

4. INPUT AND OUTPUT OF CHARACTER STRINGS

To read in or to write variable character data, the A edit descriptor of the general form

$$Aw$$

is used in a FORMAT statement (see Chapter 5 for the discussion of formatted input/output).

The field width w here is the number of characters being read in or written out.

As described in the previous section, a single memory location of a given computer, corresponding to a single variable or array element, may hold a fixed number n of characters.

The following rules hold:

(1) If w = n, all w characters are placed into the variable during input or written out from it during output.

(2) If w < n
   (a) during input, the characters are placed in the leftmost w positions of the variable, with the remaining (n − w) positions filled with blanks;
   (b) during output, the characters in the w leftmost positions in the variable are transferred.

(3) If w > n
   (a) during input, only the rightmost n characters of the field containing w characters are placed in the variable;
   (b) during output, the entire contents of the variable are transferred to occupy the rightmost n positions in the field of width w whose remaining (w − n) positions on the left are blanks.

EXAMPLE 9–2

Our computer allows a maximum of two characters per location (n = 2).
(a) The following statements:

```
      READ (5,525) INIT, MIDDLE, LAST
  525 FORMAT(A2, A1, A6)
```

are used to read the card that holds, starting with its leftmost column,

```
W.C.FIELDS
```

As the result, the above three integer variables acquire the following values:

INIT HOLDS W.   MIDDLE HOLDS C☐   LAST HOLDS DS

where ☐ is a blank.

(b) The following statements:

```
    WRITE (6,593) NONS1, NONS2, NONS3
593 FORMAT(1X, A2, A1, A6, 8H,SAID HE)
```

are used to print the following values of three integer variables:

NONS1 holds IT   NONS2 holds IS   NONS3 holds SO

The printed line will read

IT I   SO,   SAID HE
2 1   6   8H

> To avoid error-prone complexity:
> (1) use integer variables and arrays to store character data;
> (2) do not use a width $w > n$;
> (3) whenever possible, place the same number of characters in a single variable (or array element) throughout the program; for example, A1, A2, or A4. If you use the A1 descriptor, the program will be executable by any computer.

To store a longer string, linear (one-dimensional) arrays are used; for example, if a 40-character string is to be stored with two characters to an array element, it may be read in using an implied-DO list (see Chapter 5–A–5):

```
    READ (5,523) (LINE(I), I = 1, 20)
523 FORMAT(20A2)
```

assuming that the entire string is contained on a single card.

5. MANIPULATION OF CHARACTER STRINGS

If a variable or an array element contains characters, its value may be meaningfully assigned to another character-valued variable or array element.

Thus, referring to Example 9–2(b), the result of the statement

```
NONS1 = NONS2
```

is the assignment of the string IS to variable NONS1.

Also, two-character strings may be compared with the use of a logical IF statement. The notion of "greater" (or "smaller") is determined in this case by the numerical representation of characters in the character code of the computer. All character codes ensure that the letters of the alphabet are in order ($A < B < \ldots < Z$), all digits are in order ($0 < 1 < \ldots 9$), and a blank is smaller than letters and digits. The ordering of the characters by their coded representations is called a collating sequence.

The following example performs the comparison of two strings. Characteristically, strings are stored in integer linear arrays and processed with the use of DO loops.

EXAMPLE 9-3

Compare two arbitrary strings to determine their equality or sequence.

The program coded in conformance with the FORTRAN IV standard is

```
C    PROGRAM: STRINGS
C    AUTHOR:            DATE:
C
C             TWO STRINGS ARE COMPARED
C      (STRINGS ARE NOT TO EXCEED 200 CHARACTERS)
C
C    FIRST - STRING
C    SECOND - STRING
C
      INTEGER FIRST(200), SECOND(200)
C    READ IN AND ECHO BOTH STRINGS, POSSIBLY WITH TRAILING BLANKS
      READ (5,501) (FIRST(I), I = 1, 200)
  501 FORMAT(80A1)
      READ (5,501) (SECOND(I), I = 1, 200)
      WRITE (6,502) (FIRST(I), I = 1, 200)
  502 FORMAT(1X, 100A1)
      WRITE (6,502) (SECOND(I), I = 1, 200)
C
C    COMPARE STRINGS UNTIL FIRST DISTINGUISHING CHARACTER
C     IS ENCOUNTERED
      DO 10 I = 1, 200
          IF (FIRST(I) .LT. SECOND(I)) GOTO 20
          IF (FIRST(I) .GT. SECOND(I)) GOTO 30
   10 CONTINUE
C
      WRITE (6, 503)
  503 FORMAT(/ ' STRINGS ARE EQUAL')
      STOP
   20 CONTINUE
      WRITE (6, 504)
  504 FORMAT(/ ' FIRST STRING PRECEDES SECOND')
      STOP
   30 WRITE (6, 505)
  505 FORMAT(/ ' FIRST STRING FOLLOWS SECOND')
      STOP
      END
```

Here are the results of two sample runs.

run 1:

```
        THIS IS THE FIRST STRING  ⎫
                                  ⎬ input strings
        THIS IS THE SECOND STRING ⎭


    FIRST STRING PRECEDES SECOND
```

run 2:

```
        THIS  IS  THE  SECOND  STRING

        THIS  IS  THE  SECOND  STRING

    STRINGS  ARE  EQUAL
```

In some programming problems, the length of the string may change as a result of its processing, for example, due to the replacement of a part of the string—a substring—by a longer one. In these cases, the current length of the string has to be maintained as a separate integer variable in order to, for example, write out the string from the array that holds it.

B. STRING PROCESSING WITH CHARACTER DATA IN FORTRAN 77

FORTRAN 77 introduced character data as a distinct type, thus enabling the programmer to declare character variables, arrays, and functions. The essential operation defined on strings is their concatenation; another operation possible is the extraction of a substring from a string. A number of intrinsic functions are provided to simplify string processing.

At the same time, FORTRAN 77 makes it possible to use implicit string processing methods, described in Section A of this chapter. This makes for portability of programs conforming to the old standard. With the facilities described here available, the programmer does not, however, normally resort to the embedding of character data in variables (or arrays) of other types.

1. CHARACTER CONSTANTS

A character constant is a sequence (string) of one or more characters enclosed in apostrophes (single quotes), e.g.,

```
'JOHN'    ''    'HERE IS'    '2+2=4'    'CAN''T'
```

The two delimiting apostrophes are not a part of the string.

As shown in the last example above, whenever an apostrophe is contained in the string itself, it is to be represented by the programmer as a double apostrophe.

2. HOW TO DECLARE ENTITIES OF THE CHARACTER TYPE

To declare variables, arrays, or functions whose value is a character string, the CHARACTER type statement is used. In FORTRAN, every character-valued entity must have a fixed length (number of characters), specified by the programmer in the appropriate CHARACTER statement.

The CHARACTER statement has the following general form:

CHARACTER list of variable, array, and/or function names, with their length specifications

The length of each entity, i.e., the number of characters in its value, must be specified in this list by *N, where N is an integer constant greater than 0. If the CHARACTER statement has an "overall" length specification following the keyword CHARACTER, it applies to each entity without its own length. If no length specification at all is given for an entity, its length is assumed to be 1; for example,

CHARACTER *10 FIRST, MIDDLE *2, LAST, JOBS(5) *20

As a type statement, the CHARACTER statement may be used to declare dimensions of arrays. For arrays, the length of each element is specified (thus, arrays always consist of elements of equal length). The "overall" length specification may be optionally followed by a comma.

EXAMPLE 9-4

(a)

CHARACTER *10 FIRST, MIDDLE *2, LAST, JOBS(5) *20

declares
   variables FIRST and LAST of length 10;
   variable MIDDLE of length 2;
   array JOBS with five elements, each having the length 20.

(b)

CHARACTER HE, SHE

declares variables HE and SHE of length 1 each.

The CHARACTER type statement is placed before all executable statements (usually, among other type statements).

The length of the entity does not change during program execution.†

Once declared in a CHARACTER statement, an entity may not be assigned a numeric value or be used as an operand in a numeric expression.

The dimensions of a character-valued array may be declared in a separate DIMENSION statement (but not in both the DIMENSION and the CHARACTER statements). The type of a character-valued function may instead be declared in its FUNCTION statement.

---

† Owing to this, memory allocation in FORTRAN may be performed statically (by the compiler), since the number of locations needed to store all the program data is known before the execution starts.

PROCESSING OF CHARACTER STRINGS & LOGICAL DATA

An IMPLICIT statement (see Chapter 4–B) may be used to declare that all the names of variables, arrays, and functions beginning with a given letter are of the CHARACTER type and of the given length; e.g.,

```
IMPLICIT CHARACTER *10 (A-Z)
```

In a function or a subroutine subprogram, the length of a dummy argument may be left unspecified by being declared with the symbols (*). In such a case, the length of the corresponding actual argument will be used following the invocation of the subprogram. Also, the length of a character-valued function may be left similarly unspecified; it has to be, however, specified in the program unit that invokes the function.

EXAMPLE 9–5

The main program contains the following statements:

```
CHARACTER *50 STRING, INVERT, NEXT



NEXT = INVERT(STRING)
```

This program unit invokes a function that inverts the order of characters in the variable STRING:

```
CHARACTER *(*) FUNCTION INVERT(ORIGIN)
CHARACTER ORIGIN *(*)
```

Thus, a string of any length may be processed by the function (where it is called ORIGIN). The inverted string will be assigned to the function name, INVERT.

If a character variable or array is to be placed in a COMMON block, the entire block may contain exclusively character entities.

3. INPUT AND OUTPUT OF CHARACTER STRINGS

For the formatted input and output of character strings, we use the A edit descriptor discussed in Section A–4 of this chapter.

However, in the case of CHARACTER type data, the length of a character-valued variable is not limited by the capacity of a single memory word. The length of such a variable or array element is defined in the appropriate CHARACTER declaration and is to be, in general, matched by the width field w and Aw (unless the data are to be read or written partially).

EXAMPLE 9-6

To input the value of the variable NAME declared

```
CHARACTER *25 NAME
```

we will use

```
      READ (5,511) NAME
 511 FORMAT(A25)
```

or

```
 511 FORMAT(A20)
```

provided that the name is placed in the 20 leftmost columns of the data card.

List-directed input and output, which do not require the use of a FORMAT, may be used in FORTRAN 77 (see Chapter 4–D). In this case, the programmer has no control over the layout of printed data; it is fixed for the given implementation.

4. MANIPULATION OF STRINGS

Character variables and array elements may be initialized with a DATA statement (see Chapter 6–B); for example,

```
CHARACTER NAME *4, TABLE(3, 10) *7
DATA NAME/'JOHN'/, TABLE/30*'NOTHING'/
```

Character variables and array elements may be assigned a value in an assignment statement; for example,

```
NAME = 'JOHN'
```

or

```
NAME = FIRST
```

assuming that FIRST is also a character variable.

If the value of a "shorter" variable is assigned to a "longer" variable, it is padded on the right with blanks. If, conversely, a "longer" value is assigned to a "shorter" variable, extra characters on the right are dropped.

EXAMPLE 9-7

Variables NAME1 and NAME2 are declared as follows:

```
CHARACTER NAME1 *6, NAME2 *2
```

Following the execution of the assignment statements

```
NAME1 = 'JOHN'
NAME2 = 'JOHN'
```

the value of NAME1 is 'JOHN☐☐', and the value of NAME2 is 'JO'.

Two character strings may be joined together by the *concatenation operator* // (double slashes).

> **EXAMPLE 9-8**
>
> If the value of FIRST is 'JOHN', following the execution of the assignment statement
>
>   NAME = FIRST // ' SMITH'
>
> the value of NAME is 'JOHN SMITH' (provided that the length of NAME is 10).

A *substring* is a continuous part of a string. A substring name is formed as follows:

character variable name (beginning : end),
e.g.,

    NAME(2:4)

or

character array element name (beginning : end),
e.g.,

    LINE(3) (15:20)

The "beginning" and the "end" are the positions of the first and last character of the substring within the string; they must be positive integer constants or integer expressions that evaluate to such constants. Their values should satisfy the following inequality:

$1 \leqslant$ beginning $\leqslant$ end $\leqslant$ length of the string

If the values of the beginning and the end are equal, they refer to a single character.

> **EXAMPLE 9-9**
>
> Assuming that the value of variable OFFER is 'CUP OF TEA', and the value of I is 8:
>   the value of OFFER(5:6) is 'OF';
>   the value of OFFER(3:3) is 'P';
>   the value of OFFER(I:I+2) is 'TEA'.

A substring name may appear on either side of an assignment statement. In this fashion, a substring of a string may be replaced by another substring of the same length.

EXAMPLE 9-10

(a) Using the variable OFFER of Example 9-9, with the assignment statement

```
OFFER(1:3) = 'MUG'
```

we produce the new value of OFFER, which is 'MUG OF TEA'.

(b) Assuming that the value of OFFER is 'CUP OF TEA' and TEMP is a character variable of length 3, the following sequence of statements

```
TEMP = OFFER(8:10)
OFFER(8:10) = OFFER(1:3)
OFFER(1:6) = TEMP // ' IN'
```

produces a new value of OFFER, namely, 'TEA IN CUP'.

If a substring is to be replaced by another of a different length, a DO loop is used to move the characters on the right-hand side of the replacement to the left (if the new string is shorter) or to the right (if the new string is longer). Of course, the length of the variable that holds the string should be no shorter than the new, longer, string.

Using the concatenation operator, character entities, and intrinsic functions with character arguments (see next section), we may build *character expressions* that may appear on the right-hand side of a character assignment statement (see Example 9-10).

The following restriction applies to the character assignment statements: no character position that is being assigned a value may appear on the right-hand side of the assignment statement. This means, for example, that the following assignment statement is illegal:

```
OFFER(1:5) = OFFER(5:10)
```

since the position 5 appears on both sides of the assignment statement.

Two character strings may be compared with the use of the same relational operators that are used to compare numerical values; thus, conditions may be formed and employed in logical IF statements (see Chapter 7-D) for comparison of character values.

EXAMPLE 9-11

The availability of character variables of an arbitrary specified length simplifies programming. For example, if two strings are specified as follows:

```
CHARACTER *200 FIRST, SECOND
```

the DO loop of Example 9–3 may be replaced by:

```
            IF (FIRST .LT. SECOND) GOTO 20
            IF (FIRST .GT. SECOND) GOTO 30
  C    STRINGS ARE EQUAL
            .
            .
            .
  C    FIRST STRING PRECEDES SECOND
       20 CONTINUE
            .
            .
            .
  C    FIRST STRING FOLLOWS SECOND
       30 CONTINUE
            .
            .
            .
```

As already explained, characters are represented with the use of a character code in which a distinct bit pattern corresponds to every representable character. Such a code establishes a collating sequence of characters: their order of precedence in terms of their binary representation. Thus, character strings may be compared (and sorted, if necessary) like ordinary integers. Any collating sequence is appropriate for FORTRAN string processing, so long as all letters of the alphabet are in order, all digits are in order, and a blank precedes ("is smaller than") the letters and the digits.

Two character codes are used most frequently (depending on the computer model): ASCII and EBCDIC. In ASCII, the collating sequence is in increasing order; blank, digits, characters; in EBCDIC: blank, characters, digits.

EXAMPLE 9–12

In any character code recognized by the FORTRAN 77 system:

'THIS' .LT. 'THAT' has the value .FALSE.;
'7' .GT. '3' has the value .TRUE.;
'BLANK ' .LT. 'BLANKS' has the value .TRUE.;
'21' .GT. '54' has the value .FALSE..

Additionally, intrinsic functions are provided for comparison of strings in the ASCII collating sequence, independent of the actual character code used in the given computer model. These functions, discussed in the next section, may be used instead of relational operators to ensure that the program is portable among various computer models.

5. INTRINSIC FUNCTIONS FOR STRING MANIPULATION

A number of intrinsic (built-in, see Chapter 6–C) functions are provided in FORTRAN 77 to operate on arguments of character type.

The function

$$\text{LEN(character expression)}$$

computes the length of the string represented by the character expression.
The function

$$\text{INDEX}(C_1, C_2)$$

locates the position of the string C_2 in the string C_1. In general, both C_2 and C_1 may be character expressions.
The function

$$\text{INDEX}$$

(1) returns an integer value, indicating the starting position of C_2 in C_1 if it appears there as a substring.
(2) If C_2 occurs in C_1 more than once, the position of the leftmost occurrence is indicated.
(3) If C_2 does not occur in C_1, the function returns the value 0.

EXAMPLE 9–13

(a)

    LEN ('THIS IS A STRING')

returns the value 16.
If we assume that the value of the variable OFFER is
'CUP OF TEA', then

    LEN (OFFER)

has the value of 10;

    LEN ('BIG ' //OFFER)

has the value of 14.

(b)

    INDEX('TARTAN', 'TAN')

equals 4;

    INDEX('TARTAN', 'TA')

equals 1;
If OFFER has the value 'CUP OF TEA',

    INDEX(OFFER, 'COFFEE')

equals 0.

Four intrinsic functions are provided to supplant the relational operators. They compare the string values "lexically," according to the ASCII collating sequence, i.e., without regard to the computer model. The two arguments C_1 and C_2 of each of these functions may be any character expressions.

These functions are presented in Table 9–1; the acronym LGE, for example, stands for "lexically greater or equal."

TABLE 9–1. Intrinsic functions for lexical comparison.

INTRINSIC FUNCTION	RETURNS THE VALUE .TRUE. IF
$LGE(C_1, C_2)$	string C_1 equals or follows string C_2
$LGT(C_1, C_2)$	string C_1 follows string C_2
$LLE(C_1, C_2)$	string C_1 equals or precedes string C_2
$LLT(C_1, C_2)$	string C_1 precedes string C_2

If the operands are of unequal length, the shorter operand is considered as if it were extended to the right with blanks to match the length of the longer operand.

EXAMPLE 9–14

Assuming that the value of the character variable NAME is 'JOHN',
(a) the statement

```
IF (LLT(NAME, 'PETER')) GOTO 40
```

will cause a transfer of control;
(b) the statement

```
IF (LGE(NAME, 'JILL')) GOTO 20
```

will also cause control transfer.

The following example illustrates character manipulation.

EXAMPLE 9–15

```
C   THE FUNCTION DETERMINES THE LENGTH OF A STRING
C   WITHOUT THE TRAILING BLANKS
        INTEGER FUNCTION NUMCHR(STRING)
        CHARACTER STRING *(*)
C   SEARCH FROM RIGHT FOR THE FIRST NON-BLANK
        DO 10 NUMCHR = LEN(STRING), 1, −1
            IF (STRING(NUMCHR:NUMCHR) .NE. ' ') GOTO 20
    10 CONTINUE
    20 RETURN
        END
```

Observe how the length is returned as the value of the function name.

C. LOGICAL DATA AND THEIR PROCESSING

To express conditions on which the flow of control in a program is predicated we use logical expressions (see Chapter 7–D–2). These expressions can assume only one of two values: .TRUE. or .FALSE..

In FORTRAN, logical constants, variables, arrays, and functions may be declared and manipulated with the use of logical operations.

There are only two logical constants (and thus two values of logical variables and array elements); these are written in FORTRAN as

.TRUE. and .FALSE.

To declare a logical variable or array, the following type statement is used:

LOGICAL list of variable, array and/or function names

As usual, arrays may be fully specified in a type statement; for example,

LOGICAL ANSWER, QUIZ(10, 20)

The essential tool for the manipulation of logical data is the assignment statement of the following form:

$$\left.\begin{array}{c} \text{logical variable} \\ \text{or} \\ \text{element of logical array} \end{array}\right\} = \text{logical expression}$$

Logical expressions are formed and evaluated according to the rules explained in Chapter 7–D–2. These expressions include, in the order of precedence, the following operators:

arithmetic;
relational: .LT., .LE., .EQ., .NE., .GE., .GT.;
logical: .NOT., .AND., .OR.

The truth table for the logical operators is presented as Table 7–2.

▷ FORTRAN 77 includes two additional logical operators: .EQV. and .NEQV., of which the latter is known in logic as *exclusive - or,* and the former is its inverse (logical equivalence).   ◁

A logical variable may be initialized with a DATA statement; for example,

LOGICAL PRED
DATA PRED/.FALSE./

A logical function may be defined; for example,

LOGICAL FUNCTION TEST(X, Y)

For the input and output of logical values, the Lw edit descriptor is used (see Chapter 5 for the general discussion of formatted I/O), where w is the length of the field occupied by the data item.

On input, the leading character in this field must be the letter T (for TRUE) or F (for FALSE), optionally preceded by blanks and a period. Thus, one may use .TRUE. and .FALSE. (or T and F if space is being conserved) to read in the desired values.

On output, (w −1) blanks, followed by the letter T or F, will be presented.

Logical data are used, as explained before, to control the flow of execution. In certain problems, however, the presentation of program data in the form of logical data appears more natural; moreover, storage and manipulation time may be reduced in comparison with integer representations. The following example illustrates such use of logical data.

EXAMPLE 9-16

Problem
Students have responded to a "yes-no" quiz of 20 questions; each correct answer is worth 5 points. A grading program is to be designed to process the responses.

Solution
The responses of every student are encoded on a single card. This card is compared with the master card with correct responses, and the total score for each student is arrived at.

Pseudocode of the Algorithm

```
*GRADING
begin
      Input correct answers;
      while there are more student cards do
          begin
              Input next student card;
              SCORE ← 0;
              while less than 20 answers do
                  if answer is correct then
                          SCORE ← SCORE + 5
                  else;
                  Output student ID, answers, SCORE
          end
end
```

PROGRAM

```
C    PROGRAM: GRADING
C    AUTHOR:            DATE:
C
C    STUDENT ANSWERS ARE GRADED ACCORDING TO THE MASTER
C
C    MASTER(I) - CORRECT ANSWERS
C    ANSWRS(I) - STUDENT ANSWERS
C    STDID - STUDENT ID NUMBER
C    SCORE - STUDENT'S SCORE
C
     INTEGER STDID, SCORE
     LOGICAL MASTER(50), ANSWRS(50)
C
C    INPUT MASTER WITH CORRECT ANSWERS
     READ (5,501) (MASTER(I), I = 1,20)
 501 FORMAT(20L1)
C    PRINT HEADER
     WRITE (6,502)
 502 FORMAT('1',4X, 'STUDENT ID', 19X, 'ANSWERS', 25X, 'SCORE'/)
C
C    INPUT AND GRADE STUDENT ANSWERS
  10 READ (5,503, END = 30) STDID, (ANSWRS(I), I = 1,20)
 503     FORMAT(I10, 20L1)
         SCORE = 0
         DO 20 I = 1,20
             IF ((ANSWRS(I) .AND. MASTER(I)) .OR.
     +          (.NOT. ANSWRS(I) .AND. .NOT. MASTER(I)))
     +          SCORE = SCORE + 5
  20     CONTINUE
         WRITE (6,504) STDID, (ANSWRS(I), I = 1,20), SCORE
 504     FORMAT(5X, I10, 5X, 20L2, I10)
     GOTO 10
  30 STOP
     END
```

The printout corresponding to this master

```
T T T T T F F F F F T T T T T F F F F F
```

is

STUDENT ID	ANSWERS	SCORE
378976545	T T T T T T T T T T T T T T T T T T T T	50
456435678	F F F F T T T T T F F F F F T T T T T T	0
300047562	F F F F F F F F F F F F F F F F F F F F	50
156789230	T T T T T F F F F F T T T T T F F F F F	100

SUGGESTED FURTHER READING

An advanced text on FORTRAN programming is

Hughes, C. E., Pfleeger, C. P., and Rose, L. L.: *Advanced Programming Techniques—A Second Course in Programming Using FORTRAN*, Wiley, New York, 1978.

To gain deeper understanding of programming constructs and computer systems, the student may use

Zwass, V.: *Introduction to Computer Science*, Barnes & Noble, New York, 1981.

Important matters of programming style and ensuring program correctness are discussed in

Kernighan, B. W., and Plauger, P. J.: *The Elements of Programming Style*, 2nd ed., McGraw-Hill, New York, 1978.

Ledgard, H. F., and Chmura, L. J.: *FORTRAN with style*, Hayden, Rochelle Park, N.J., 1978.

Van Tassel, D.: *Program Style, Design, Efficiency, Debugging, and Testing*, 2nd ed., Prentice-Hall, Englewood Cliffs, N.J., 1978.

As sources of many programming problems, with discussion and solution aids, may serve

Teague, R.: *Computing Problems for FORTRAN Solutions*, Harper & Row, San Francisco, 1972.

Maurer, H. A., and Williams, M. R.: *A Collection of Programming Problems and Techniques*, Prentice-Hall, Englewood Cliffs, N.J., 1972.

INDEX